LOCOMOTION PAPERS

Railways to Skegness

including

Kirkstead to Little Steeping

by
A.J. Ludlam

THE OAKWOOD PRESS

© Oakwood Press & A.J. Ludlam, 1997

British Library Cataloguing in Publication Data
A Record for this book is available from the British Library
ISBN 0 85361 518 7

Typeset by Oakwood Graphics.
Repro by Ford Graphics, Ringwood, Hants.
Printed by Alpha Print (Oxford) Ltd, Witney, Oxon.

Dedicated to Charles Sharp and the efforts of SELTA in its continuing struggle to protect the rail links to Skegness.

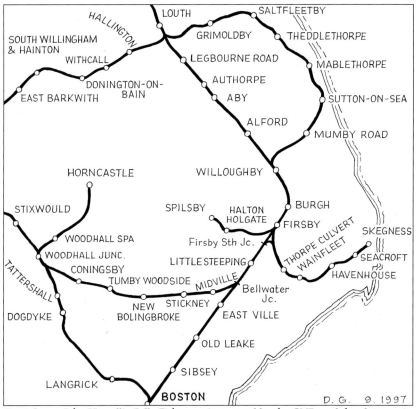

Front Cover: John Hassall's 'Jolly Fisherman' was used by the GNR, and then later, as in this version, by the LNER to promote tourist traffic to Skegness.
National Railway Museum/Skegness Town Council/Science & Society Picture Library
Rear Cover: A postcard from the early part of the century. *Author's Collection*
Title Page: An early bird's eye view of Skegness.

Published by
The Oakwood Press
P.O. Box 13, Usk, Mon, NP5 1YS.

Contents

A view of the first station at Skegness prior to the doubling of the line.

Winston Kime Collection

Perhaps the best-known of all British railway posters. John Hassall's 'Jolly Fisherman' skipping along the beach. The 'Jolly Fisherman' was first adopted by the Great Northern Railway' but the image continued to be used well into LNER days.

National Railway Museum/Skegness Town Council/Science & Society Picture Library

Introduction

Come, bretheren of the water
And let us all assemble
To treat this matter, which
Doth make us quake and tremble;
For we shall rue, if it be true,
That the Fens be undertaken,
And where we feed, in fen and reed
They'll feed both beef and bacon

Charles Kingsley, expressing sympathy with the Fensmen in their struggle against enclosure of the Fens.

An understanding of the Lincolnshire Fens is an understanding of the struggle to control water, the threat from which manifested itself in three particular ways; the sea; inundation from higher ground to the west; and rain. It was drainage that allowed land in the Fens to be settled and used. The modern Fen landscape is man-made, with a history as old as humanity. Early efforts to control the Fenlands was often piecemeal and frequently disastrous. It was not until the 19th century that man began to take overall control of the area, making it safer to farm and live in. At this time the majority of farming was carried out on permanent pasture, sheep and cattle dominated. Today the area is down to arable farming. It is difficult nowadays to comprehend the massive fundamental changes that have taken place in the Fens over the past centuries. Although the Fens spread over a huge area from Huntingdon to South Lincolnshire, the districts that concern us were known as East, West and Wildmore Fens, in south Lincolnshire. Because of the huge changes that took place in creating the area through which the two railways, which are our particular interest, ran, I thought it appropriate to give a brief account of the transformation, especially as so many of the engineers associated with the drainage of the region were also intimately involved in the development of railways throughout the country.

The Kirkstead to Little Steeping and the Firsby to Skegness railways both link-in with other titles by me published by the Oakwood Press, *The East Lincolnshire Railway* and the *Lincolnshire Loop Line*. Areas that are dealt with in detail in these two volumes, for example Boston, will only be touched upon here.

A.J. Ludlam
Grimsby, 1997

Fenman hunting wildfowl.

The fens - Wainfleet and Skegness.

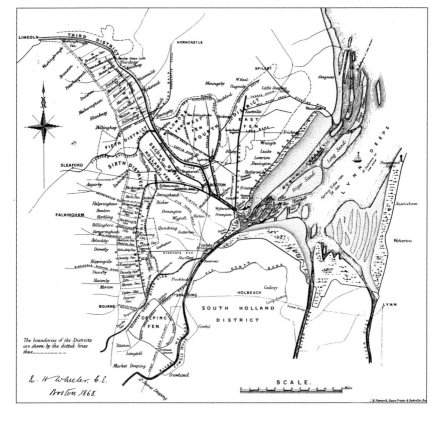

Chapter One

The Lincolnshire Fens

From the various remains of trees found buried beneath the Fens it is reckoned that in prehistoric times this was a heavily wooded area, with the remains of oak, alder, birch, yew and others in evidence. In later times trees were less in evidence, only the elm managing to achieve any kind of growth. Whitethorn hedges flourished, achieving a great height and size.

It is generally assumed that the Fens in pre-Roman times was a vast morass into which the waters of the Trent, Witham, Welland, Nene and Ouse emptied. Being below the level of high-tides the area was constantly invaded by the sea. As the land rose by virtue of alluvial deposits and vegetation began to appear, large free-flowing creeks became stagnant pools. Islands of high ground supported small groups of inhabitants whose contact with the mainland was by coracle. In Julius Caesar's account of Britain it is stated that the Fen coast was peopled by Belgae, 'drawn thither by the love of war and plunder'.

The tribe of Britons who occupied the Fenlands were known as Iceni - from the word Ychen, or oxen. They lived almost entirely on flesh, milk and birds, the higher land providing good feeding grounds for their herds. Lindcoit (Lincoln) was the principal town and Bardney the main Druidical centre.

The Romans were responsible for the construction of a 50 mile-long sea bank running along the coast and protecting the Fens from the invading sea. These are still referred to as 'Roman Banks'. This was a major engineering feat by any standards, requiring a vast army of men and superb organisation. A powerful motive for the Romans undertaking this work was that it helped in their attempts to dislodge the natives, who Hercullinus described as 'not dwelling in towns but in cottages in fenny places compassed by thick woods having hidden whatsoever they had most estimation of, did more annoyance to the wearied Romans than they received from them'.

There was a Roman station at Vainona (Wainfleet), Wainfleet Haven at that time, being the only place on the coast where Roman vessels could ride safely and find protection. Wainfleet was the main landing place for their station at Lincoln. A road from Wainfleet to Lincoln passed through Irby, Steeping, Spilsby, Winceby, Baumber, Wragby, Sudbrooke, Holme and Langworth to Lincoln. The road also linked Wainfleet to Horncastle with a branch to the Roman station at Burgh. The name Wainfleet evolved from the Anglo-Saxon words, 'Wayn'- marshland 'Fleet' - a tidal creek.

When the Romans withdrew from Britain Saxon colonists soon took possession of the Fens and almost completely wiped out all evidence of the Romano-British presence. The Anglo-Saxons defended the Fens against all comers, indeed the Norman conquerors became absorbed into Fen culture rather than vice-versa.

The general condition of the Fens remained unaltered for about 500 years. Flooding and inundations were frequently recorded. In 1394, . . .

. . . the marshes of East and West Fenne as also divers lands, meadows and pastures lying in the towns of Leek, Wrangle, Friskeneye and Waynflete betwixt the waters of the Witham and Waynflete were drowned by a great inundation of water, so that all the inhabitants of those towns did wholly lose benefit of their lands and marshes there through the defects of a certain floodgate at Waynflete, which was so narrow that the course of the waters passing that way could not get to the sea.

The establishment of the Court of Sewers during the reign of Henry VIII saw several ineffective efforts made to improve the condition of the Fens. Both the Crown, and later a group called the Adventurers, failed in their efforts to reclaim the Fens, due principally to the lawlessness of the Fenmen who wrecked sluices and filled in drains.

It was from the numerous birds and fishes that the Fenmen obtained their living and it was this way of life that they defended so forcefully. With the inclosure of the Fens many species of birds disappeared. Lincolnshire was described as the aviary of England, the wildfowl remarkable for their plenty, so much so that 'in the month of August 3,000 mallards and others of that kind, were caught in one draught', their variety 'there being scarce enough names for the several kinds' and their deliciousness, 'wild fowl being more dainty than some because of their continual motion'.

In Percy's *Household Book* of 1512 the value of birds is given as: lapwings, knutes and dotterells one penny each; sea gulls, plovers, woodcocks and redshanks one penny ha'penny each; pigeons, terns and snipes three for a penny; ruffs and partridges twopence each; bitterns and curlews one penny ha'penny each.

No less than 77 inland fisheries were shown to be paying rent in the Domesday Book. Some rents were paid in fish, for instance the market town of Bourne paid 2,500 eels a year. The salt water fishery the Boston Deeps was of great value, the Romans sent oysters from here to Rome. Mussels were in demand as live bait in the ports of the North of England. Often more than 50 vessels would move more than 1,000 tons in one season, carrying them to Bridlington, Scarborough and other northern ports. After the opening of the Great Northern Railway, in 1848, this trade was transferred to the railway and was further extended to Eyemouth and the Scottish ports. In 1853 one hundred tons a week was being exported. In 1873, during the months of November and December, 1,134 tons were despatched by rail from Boston.

Cockles were another lucrative trade employing about 100 men and boys in their collection. The cockles were formerly sent out in their shells, but later were put into hot water to remove their shells. They were salted and sent out by rail to the large towns. In 1889, 54,630 cwt of cockles worth £2,237 were landed at Boston. By 1893 this had peaked at 82,860 cwt, at a value of £5,671. These weights included shells.

From the earliest times the Fens were well provided with the means of transporting produce from the land to market. The Romans not only provided roads from the coast to the interior but also navigable waterways throughout the Fens. In the area that concerns us, the Witham and Wainfleet Haven afforded a means of communication with the sea and different parts of the district.

The Great Northern (GNR), Great Eastern and Midland Railway Companies later added to the existing facilities.

The reclamation of the Fens to its modern day condition is due to the ingenuity of what reads like a 'Who's Who' of engineering; John Rennie, Smeaton, Telford, Labelye, Mylue, Cubitt, Brunel, Walker, Robert Stephenson, Hawkesley, Hawkshaw and Coode.

Streatfield writing in Victorian times wrote:

The vast mere, studded with the island homes of English colonists which stretched from Horncastle and Spilsby to Ramsey and Huntingdon, has disappeared and given place to the richest agricultural district in England. As we contemplate the never ending fields of corn, mustard and potato during our railway journey from Huntingdon to Firsby we can scarcely repress a sigh for the beds of osier and sedge which were so common and much more natural, though less profitable. We perhaps confess that things are better as they are; yet cannot dissemble our regret at the change . . . But while much has gone and much more is going it is a thought full of interest that so many natural objects remain to connect the present with the past. As we gather wayside flowers there is a pleasure in recollecting that they sprung from those which Britons, Romans, Saxons and Danes plucked before us . . . It may be mere sentiment, but as we near the shrill whistle of the curlew, or watch the marshalled ranks of wild geese as they fly from the salt marsh to the Wolds, we find pleasure in remembrance that Geirmund and Ulfric saw the same sights a thousand years ago.

Fen Slodgers

GREAT NORTHERN RAILWAY.

OPENING

OF THE

FIRSBY & WAINFLEET BRANCH

SERVICE OF TRAINS

From TUESDAY, 24th OCTOBER,

UNTIL FURTHER NOTICE.—

UP-WEEK DAYS.

	1,2 Pass	A Mkd.Train								Saturdays only.
WAINFLEET ...... dep.	6 54	7 26	8 35	11 0	12 50	3 50	4 35	5 20		6 10
Thorpe Culvert										
FIRSBY ...... arr.	7 7	7 39	8 48	11 13	1 3	4 3	4 48	5 33		6 23
Firsby ...... dep.		7 40				A				6 30
Alford		8 6			1 8	4 15				6 52
Louth		8 38			1 30	4 50				7 15
Grimsby		9 15			1 55	5 30				7 45
		A			2 20	6 10				
Firsby ...... dep.	7 8		11 15				4 50			8 21
Boston	7 50		12 0				5 50			
Lincoln	9 45		1 40				5 25			
Peterboro	9 45		1 40							8 10
LONDON (King's Cross)	11 50	12 38	4 0							10 10

DOWN—WEEK DAYS.

			B	7 40	9 0	Wednesdays only.	C			Saturdays only.
LONDON (King's Cross) ...... dep.				10 50						1 15	2 45
Peterboro				11 5						4 35
Lincoln		7 0		12 35						3 30
Boston		7 37		1 6						3 55
Firsby ...... arr.										6 28
Grimsby	5 40		9 40				2 20		5 0	
Louth	6 20		10 50				3 20		5 37	
Alford	6 48		11 12				4 40		6 5	
Firsby										6 25
FIRSBY ...... dep.	7 10	7 43	10 26	11 20	1 12	4 10	4 50	5 42		6 35
Thorpe Culvert										
WAINFLEET	7 23	7 56	10 40	11 33	1 25	4 23	5 3	5 55		6 48

FARES FROM WAINFLEET.

SINGLE			RETURN		
1st.	2nd.	Parly.	1st.	2nd.	3rd.

FARES FROM FIRSBY.

SINGLE			RETURN		
1st.	2nd.	Parly.	1st.	2nd.	3rd.

The first timetable for the Firsby and Wainfleet branch, 1871.

Chapter Two

The Wainfleet & Firsby Railway

The 'Lincoln, Horncastle, Spilsby and Wainfleet Haven Railway' was announced in a provisional Prospectus in August 1845. The name was quickly changed to the 'Lincoln, Wainfleet Haven and Boston Railway'. The cost of constructing the proposed line was estimated at £500,000. The proposals included a port to be constructed at Wainfleet, which was to provide an outlet for goods from Lancashire, Yorkshire and the Midlands. The Prospectus, as well as citing the horse fairs at Horncastle and Spilsby as potential revenue earners, also made reference to Skegness, 'an old and celebrated watering place on the coast near Wainfleet'. The engineer Thomas Page described the route as leaving Lincoln St Mark's station, crossing to the north bank of the Witham then running via Horncastle and Spilsby to Wainfleet and including a branch to Boston. A meeting held at the 'White Hart' in Spilsby on 1st September, 1845 resolved to progress the aims of the company.

Alliances were discussed with the 'Nottingham, Boston, Ambergate and Eastern Counties Junction Railway' and the 'Great Grimsby, Louth, Horncastle, Lincoln and Midland Junction Railway'. Such arrangements were seen as beneficial/particularly with regard to unification with those companies at Lincoln and Boston. However, the Wainfleet company's proposals for a connection between Lincoln and Horncastle was in competition with a similar proposal by the Grimsby company.

Boston Corporation made it clear to the Wainfleet company that it would oppose any railway within its borough which intended building a station and shipping facilities at a distance from the town as this, in their view, would be prejudicial to the interests of trade in the town.

Trouble concerning a fee for obtaining the levels and sections from the leveller precipitated the beginnings of serious troubles for the company. By January 1846 it was realised that the work at Wainfleet building the proposed port was well beyond the means of the company. At a meeting of company representatives at the Bull Inn, Horncastle, on 20th January, it was agreed that all lines connected with the 'Lincoln, Wainfleet Haven and Boston' and the 'Great Grimsby, Louth, Horncastle, Lincoln and Midland Junction Railway' should be amalgamated and attention focused on Wainfleet Haven, with work there proceeding as soon as possible. The Wainfleet company would either make an arrangement with the East Lincolnshire Railway (ELR) regarding the operation of the Boston section of the line or forego its own proposals in favour of that company.

The Grimsby company proposed that it should go ahead with the construction of the section of line between Lincoln and Horncastle and the Wainfleet company should build the Horncastle to Wainfleet section. It was agreed in February that the Grimsby company would pay £2,000 towards the expenses of the Wainfleet company and both would apply to Parliament for their respective sections of railway, and that in the event of default the Grimsby company would have the full and whole right to apply to make such lines as it considered proper, and that the Wainfleet company would withdraw its opposition.

There was, however, some opposition within the Grimsby company to presenting a Bill to Parliament, based upon alleged non-compliance with standing orders concerning some engineering matters. Their Engineer did not express much hope of answering the criticisms and a substantial number of shareholders felt they did not wish to incur further expense in such circumstances.

On 14th February, 1846 a meeting was held which effectively wound up the Wainfleet company. A notice dated 18th February, 1846 was posted in the *Lincoln, Rutland & Stamford Mercury* by W.C. Calthorpe of the Spilsby solicitors Bourne & Sons. The notice headed 'Lincoln, Wainfleet Haven and Boston Railway' read,

> The managing Directors of this company beg to announce to the shareholders that in consequence of errors alleged in the datum line and sections by a petition presented to the House of Commons by a competing company, they have submitted these allegations to their engineer who has not given them such confident assurances of being able to overcome them as will justify the Directors in proceeding in Parliament this session. They have therefore felt it their duty to enter into arrangements for postponing the scheme to a future session, with liberty to such shareholders as may prefer retiring from the company altogether to withdraw their deposits subject to deduction of a rateable proportion of expenses incurred which the committee will reduce to the lowest practicable amount. Immediate measures will be taken for carrying out this arrangement and ascertaining the amount per share to be returned.

A second notice invited any persons with claims against the company to present their accounts so that they could be discharged.

The Grimsby company found itself in similar circumstances and, on 15th May, announced that the company was dissolved. Meetings of the Wainfleet company continued, proposing a reduced scheme from Horncastle. However, at a meeting at the 'White Hart', Spilsby, on 23rd August, 1858 all business was reported as settled and the committee dissolved.

In the meantime in 1848 the East Lincolnshire Company had opened its line from Grimsby in the north of the county to Boston in the south. This offered advantages,

> . . . to grazers and cattle feeders of that part of Lincolnshire which supplied both London and Yorkshire markets with so large a portion of fat stock and the towns of Louth, Wainfleet, Spilsby and Alford by providing a more certain and ready transit for manufactured goods and merchandise, and cannot be estimated too highly.
> The prospective districts around these towns will also fully participate in the advantages of this communication with the manufacturing and large consuming towns of Yorkshire, to which nearly the entire produce of corn and wool from such districts is now transported by water carriages, so tedious, expensive and uncertain of delivery as materially to depress the price of produce in the markets of these towns and to place such produce at great disadvantage as compared with that of markets possessing greater facilities of transit.

The towns of Wainfleet and Spilsby saw the advantages enjoyed by the nearby market towns directly linked to the ELR, Louth, Alford, Burgh and Boston. Although cartage and omnibus facilities linked the two towns to the railway through Firsby station, feeling was increasingly that both needed a direct rail link to be able to compete on equal terms with their rivals.

The GNR ran services from Bishopgate Street, in London over the ELR to New Holland. The last train of the day was the 8.40 pm mail train from London which arrived at New Holland at 5.36 am; this service left mail and newspapers for Skegness at Burgh station. Other services were met by omnibuses from Wainfleet and Skegness. An omnibus left the Woolpack and Angel Inns in Wainfleet at 7.30 am taking passengers to and from the second up and down trains and the third down train at Firsby station. A further omnibus left Wainfleet at 1.20 pm taking passengers to the fourth down and the fifth up trains. An omnibus went from Skegness to meet the up trains at Burgh station which arrived at 11.12 am and 6.12 pm, returning to Skegness after meeting down trains arriving at Burgh at 1.07 and 6.39 pm. By the 1860s, with the steadily increasing popularity of Skegness, it was apparent that these services were totally inadequate.

Spilsby celebrated the opening of its railway on 1st May, 1868. The local press noted, in its Skegness column, 'This popular bathing place on the Lincolnshire coast is already attracting visitors, an omnibus will again run daily between the above and Burgh station and as the opening of the railway to Spilsby will afford facilities and access such as have not before existed, the inhabitants are preparing for a large influx of company.'

A public meeting was held at the Angel Inn, Wainfleet, in August 1868, to consider the proposal of a railway from Firsby station to Wainfleet and Skegness. The meeting was attended by many influential people and on a motion proposed by Mr D. Martin and seconded by Mr R.S. Booth, Mr B. Mason was unanimously invited to take the chair. Mr Bassitt, after alluding to the object of the meeting, referred to the importance of railway communication in an area so rich in agricultural produce. He felt that several of the landlords of the neighbourhood, through which the line would pass, were very favourably disposed to the proposals. He estimated that the line would be very beneficial to the town and would pay a good percentage on the capital interest in the purchase of shares.

The Engineer, Mr Gardener, from the firm of Lucas and Wilkinson, stated that he had made a very careful inspection of the country through which the proposed line would pass and he had never, in his experience, seen a district in which less engineering difficulties would have to be encountered, and where a line could be constructed at so little expense. He estimated the cost at £4,000 per mile and as the line would be 8¾ miles in length the total cost would be £35,000. This estimate was for a single line of rail. He alluded to the facilities offered by contractors for constructing the line if one third of the actual cost could be subscribed locally. He then pointed out on a map the direction the line would take and the situation of the station at Wainfleet. Mr Gardner suggested that a number of shares should be taken by those who felt interested in the undertaking, paying a deposit of £2 per share to pay the preliminary expenses.

Although in poor condition this early view of Wainfleet station shows the original signal box and goods shed. The goods shed was demolished to make way for the second platform in the 1900 doubling of the line.   *Wainfleet Museum*

An early view of Wainfleet station, certainly before the doubling of the track and possibly before the extension to Skegness. The engine shed and water tank are seen beyond the station building. On the left is the original goods shed and loading dock, both disappeared when the up platform was built in 1900. The sign on the end of the single-storey building advertises 'Melrose Whisky'.
                                                                                                                Author's Collection

Mr D. Martin suggested a resolution should be passed declaring the sentiments of the meeting; the following resolution was put to the meeting and passed without dissent:

At a public meeting duly convened on the 7th day of August 1868 pursuant to a public notice for the purpose of taking into consideration the desirability of making a railway from Firsby station to Skegness via Wainfleet, such a meeting being numerously attended by the inhabitants of the town and neighbourhood it was unanimously agreed by the undersigned that it would be most desirable that the proposed line of railway should be carried into effect and that the undersigned should use their best endeavours to secure that object and to co-operate with Messrs Lucas and Wilkinson and J. Bassitt, Solicitor, to carry out the same.

After a vote of thanks the Chairman declared the meeting concluded; a general feeling of unanimity pervaded the proceedings.

By the time the proposals reached Parliament the company was entitled 'The Wainfleet and Firsby Railway'. Its Act was obtained on 13th May, 1869, authorising it to make a railway from Firsby station on the ELR to the town of Wainfleet-All-Saints. Directors of the company were James Martin, Henry John Seals, Byron Mason, Edwin Crow and Isaac Gunson; the Engineer was Mr Lucas with Mr J. Daull as resident engineer. The company had capital of £18,000, with borrowing powers of £6,000. The GNR Board would not offer monetary assistance to the scheme but agreed to transport ballast free of charge. Rent for the use of Firsby station was to be £50 per annum for the first seven years, plus the cost of water for the Wainfleet engines. The GNR agreed to work the line for 60 per cent of the takings.

The first sod for the new railway was cut at Wainfleet on 19th April, 1870 by Mrs James Martin, who received an engraved spade from Henry Jackson, the Contractor. W.H. Lucas, the Engineer to the railway said he had no doubt that he would be able to complete the line by the first of September next.

Accountants of the GNR estimated the cost of running the Wainfleet line based upon reckonings of the Spilsby branch which was similar in length. Locomotive power was estimated at £887 15s. 0d., wages £338; stores £37 8s. 4d., engine greasing £13 17s. 4d.; horse shunting £39; clothing £12 5s. 6d.; printing and stationery £6; Railway Clearing House expenses £20; Rates and taxes £13 13s. 10d.; making a total of £1,367 10s. 0d. less the GNR's 60 per cent, £982 7s. 0d., making a sub-total of £385 3s. 0d. To this was added maintenance at £264 10s. 5d. giving a grand total of £649 13s. 5d.

Passenger fares were set at first class, 3d. per mile, second class 2d. and third class 1½d. per mile.

Leaving Firsby station the line went south-eastwards and, with a station at Thorpe Culvert, terminated at Wainfleet All Saints. The line was 4 miles 22 chains in length and laid with 73 lb rails. There were five level crossings and no bridges, the steepest gradient was 1 in 220 and the sharpest curve was of 13 chains radius. There was an engine shed at Wainfleet but no turntable, the GNR using tank engines to work the line. The line was operated by the train staff system.

Col Hutchinson from the Board of Trade and Messrs Cockshott and Johnson from the GNR were met at Firsby station by the Directors of the Wainfleet company on 18th October, 1870. Col Hutchinson inspected the line, accompanied by Messrs Lucas and Daull and Mr Jackson, the contractor. He pointed out one or two details requiring attention and indicated that once they were attended to the legal authority to open the line would be granted. He expressed his satisfaction with the manner in which the works had been completed and was particularly impressed by the efficient way the machinery in connection with the signals was executed. The *Lincoln, Rutland & Stamford Mercury* described the station as 'a neat building situated nearly opposite the church and forms a conspicuous object at the entrance to Wainfleet from Boston. · The line and buildings appear to have been constructed in a durable and workmanlike manner and reflect credit alike on the Directors and those engaged in carrying out the works in connection with the undertaking'.

The line had opened for goods traffic on 11th September, 1871, the legal authority was given for the commencement of passenger services on Monday 23rd October, the line opening the next day. The press reported the event:

Tuesday last was a day to be remembered at Wainfleet in connection with local events of the present generation. On that day the Wainfleet and Firsby railway was opened for passenger traffic and the labours of the Directors have been brought to a satisfactory conclusion so far as concerns the completion of the line. A timetable was issued announcing the first train on Tuesday at 6.45 am. Previous to that hour the neighbourhood of the station was thronged by people anxious to witness the departure of the first train. Our local antiquary, Mr Mells, succeeded in obtaining the first ticket issued which he retained and it will no doubt occupy a prominent place amongst that gentleman's interesting collection of curiosities. Punctually at the time announced, the train freighted with a goodly number of passengers and accompanied with the best wishes and hearty congratulations of the spectators, started on its way and a fervent 'God Speed' was uttered as it glided from the platform. A salute of detonating signals echoed along the line, and, as the carriages receded in the distance those assembled at the station fully realised the important fact that after months and years of arduous exertion the promoters and supporters of the company are now in a fair way of obtaining some tangible reward for their trouble and seeing their labours crowned with well merited success. In consequence of Tuesday being the autumn fair day it was not considered advisable to celebrate the opening day by a demonstration then but to defer the rejoicings for a week, therefore on Tuesday next a grand display of fireworks under the supervision of Goe of Norwich, will take place, a band of music will be in attendance and we have no doubt Wainfleet on the occasion will be *en fête*. H. Chaplin MP has contributed £5 and Colonel Amcotts MP £3 3s. 0d. towards the expenses of the proposed demonstrations.

The following Tuesday was a gala day in Wainfleet, flags were flown everywhere and Mr Isaac Gunson's residence displayed a beautiful device bearing the inscription, 'Success to the Wainfleet Railway'. At noon the Horncastle brass band paraded the streets playing lively music. A public dinner was provided at the Angel Inn and the festivities were completed by a splendid display of fireworks and an alfresco concert.

Chapter Three

The Skegness Extension

There existed a Roman shore fort at Skegness, (derived from Skeggi's ness, or headland). Part of the Roman Bank, built to protect the low-lying coast from invasion by the sea, ran between Skegness and the saltworks at Wainfleet. The small town of Skegness dealt with the importing of Baltic timber and over the centuries was in constant danger from the sea. Finally in 1526 the church and parish were submerged; for years after, the remains of ruined buildings could be seen at low tide ¾ mile out to sea. The Commissioners of Sewers built a new sea defence further inland called the Skegness and Winthorpe country bank, work on which began in 1568. In about 1670 Lord Castleton enclosed marshes between the bank and the sea with Green Bank, between the present day High Street and North Shore Road. Reclamations continued around Skegness, 400 acres in 1616 and a further 400 acres by 1627, making the area much more stable.

Joseph Dickinson was advertising accommodation for ladies and gentlemen at the Skegness Hotel, (later 'Enderbys' and finally 'The Vine') in 1772. Bathing machines appeared in 1784 and horse and pony races were taking place, opposite the hotel, by 1829. The New Hotel opened during the early 1800s, Skegness at this time being regarded as a place where quiet and comfort could be enjoyed, 'at a reasonable expense'.

White's Directory of 1856 described Skegness as :

> . . . a pleasant village and bathing place on the sea coast with its own parish about 1,644 acres of land and 366 inhabitants. It has several private lodging houses and two large, commodious hotels, which are provided with warm and cold shower baths and can each make up about 30 beds. A life boat and bathing machines are stationed on the beach, Skegness, until lately an obscure village, is rising in celebrity, both as a bathing place and a port, upwards of 6,000 tons of coal being landed here in one summer. Lord Monson is lord of the manor, but a great part of the soil belongs to the Earl of Scarborough, the heirs of C.B. Massingberd, C.T.S.B. Reynardson and a few smaller ones.

The development of modern Skegness was begun by Lord Scarborough, and in particular his agent H.V. Tippet, during the 1870s and was closely linked with the appearance of railways in the area. After the opening of the ELR in 1848, omnibuses serving Skegness hotels met trains at Burgh station. Even the opening of the Wainfleet & Firsby Railway did little to change Skegness' reputation as a 'village free from bustle'. The opening of the Skegness extension of the Wainfleet & Firsby changed all that. The first plots of the new town were laid out in 1873 and by 1880 a pier, pleasure gardens and a cricket ground had been provided. Soon afterwards swimming baths were built, the addition of a parish church, waterworks and drainage, a network of streets, Methodist chapels and a school began to transform the town. Lord Scarborough was a leading shareholder in companies providing many of the amenities.

The Wainfleet & Firsby applied for its Skegness extension on 6th November,

1871, and the Act was obtained on 18th July, 1872. The company was empowered to raise £27,000 new capital with borrowing powers of £9,000. A single line ran from an end-on connection at Wainfleet, 5 miles 2 chains to a terminus at Skegness. Laid with 70 lb Vignoles rails the steepest gradient was 1 in 374 and the sharpest curve was 15 chains in radius. Stations were provided at Croft Bank, Cow Bank and Skegness; there was a road level crossing at the east end of Wainfleet station and two underbridges. The station at Skegness accounted for 30 per cent of the gross cost of the line. A turntable was installed and, in anticipation of considerable excursion traffic, six carriage sidings and four platforms were provided. To help defray its costs the Wainfleet & Firsby tried to persuade the GNR to reduce the agreed 60 per cent of the takings for the working of the Wainfleet section to 50 per cent for the whole line: despite extended negotiations the request was rejected.

The extended line was opened on 28th July, 1873; single fare tickets were issued for return journeys on Mondays and Fridays.

An extremely rare view of Skegness station taken about 1880 and showing the original buildings and four platforms as well as some interesting coaching stock in platform 4.
Winston Kime Collection

Chapter Four

Traffic in the Early Days

Prior to the opening of the 'New Line', in 1913, traffic for Skegness was worked through Boston and over the ELR. In 1858 the GNR advertised excursions to Skegness from stations in Lincolnshire: tickets were for Burgh station and from there by 'conveyance' to Skegness, and were issued for up to 28 days, 'until further notice', on Monday, Thursday and Saturday only.

	1st class		2nd class	
	s.	d.	s.	d.
Louth	3	6	2	9
Boston	4	0	3	0
Tattershall	6	0	4	9
Spalding	6	6	5	0
Peterborough	9	6	7	0
Grantham	15	0	11	6
Nottingham	15	0	11	6
Lincoln	6	6	5	0
Horncastle	6	6	5	0

The opening of the Skegness extension realised an immediate increase of visitors to the seaside, or 'trippers' as they became known. In 1873 the GNR advertised the following excursions to Skegness:

On Tuesday 12th August, a cheap excursion, at excursion fares, will leave Bourn at 8.00 am, Morton 8.07, Rippingale 8.15, Billingborough 8.25, Scredington 8.35, Sleaford 8.50, Heckington 9.00, Swineshead 9.09, Hubberts Bridge 9.20, Boston 9.30, Firsby 10.15 and Wainfleet at 10. 30. Returning from Skegness the same day at 7.30 pm.

On Saturday 9th August, a cheap excursion will leave Lincoln at 8.30 am, Washingborough 8.35, Bardney 8.50, Horncastle 8.30, Woodhall Spa 8.40, Kirkstead 9.05 and 9.35, Boston 9.45 and 10.05, Firsby 10.15 and 10.42 and Wainfleet at 10.30. Returning from Skegness on the same day at only 7.30 pm.

On Monday 11th August a cheap excursion will leave Peterborough at 6.15 am, Peakirk 6.25, St James Deeping 6.30, Littleworth 6.38, March 6.00, Guyhirne 6.07, Murrow 6.13, French Drove 6.19, Postland 6.26, Cowbit 6.34, Sutton Bridge 6.00, Long Sutton 6.07, Gedney 6.09, Fleet 6.14, Holbeach 6.22, Moulton 6.33, Spalding 6.50, Surfleet 6.57, Algarkirk 7.05, Kirton 7.10, Boston 7.20. Returning from Skegness at 7.30 pm.

In May 1875 a train was chartered from Kirkstead, taking 200 people to the seaside and in July 925 children from the Wesleyan Sunday School, in Horncastle, had a day at Skegness. The Skegness races of 1876 were attended by 12,000 people, the GNR providing cheap excursions.

The book of records of Spilsby Church gives details of a trip to the seaside for Sunday School children on 10th July, 1877:

Took place on a day that was beautifully fine, over 100 children with their teachers assembled for prayers at the National School at 10.00 am, after which they marched to the station headed by the Spilsby Drum and Fife Band, who kindly gave their services for the day.

Here the train was taken for Skegness where a long and enjoyable day was spent, teachers and friends doing all in their power to afford pleasure to the younger ones. A capital dinner of beef sandwiches was provided for all at one o' clock by Mrs Clifton at the Vine and cake and tea at four o' clock, after which some of the smaller children returned home, the bigger ones stayed till the mail train.

Before leaving the Vine three hearty cheers were given for Mrs Clifton, the teachers and the vicar. About 70 parents and friends availed themselves of the cheap fare, kindly granted by the GNR company, 6½d. each for the return journey.

The account for the outing.

	£	s.	d.
Receipts in hand		15	7½
Subscriptions for the treat	5	15	6
	6	11	1½
Balance	10	0	5
Payments			
130 Railway fares for children, teachers and Band	3	10	5
Mrs Clifton for dinners and teas	6	10	0

Day excursion traffic continued to increase with 22,000 visitors in 1887. In June 1880 an excursion train of 38 carriages transported 1,000 scholars of the Blue Coat School in Lincoln and on 3rd July over 12,000 passengers arrived at the resort. The 8th July saw the arrival of a train carrying 700 people associated with the choirs of St Mary's Church and the Trinity Chapel in Horncastle; included was the band of the Horncastle Volunteers who entertained at Boston station and Skegness.

Although the resort continued to grow in size, the impact of these invasions upon the resident population of just over 1,000 people must have been profound and is delightfully described by the local press of the time, 'excursionists drop down upon the place in numbers so overwhelming as to leave the town as bare of nutriment as was Egypt after the visitation of the locusts', also the habits of some of the excursionists, 'especially the ladies and gentlemen from Sheffield and Oldham', were considered rather primitive, 'they think nothing of walking into a lady's parlour and informing the astonished resident that they would 'loike t'ave some beer'. And further that, 'both sexes bathe together in hundreds and flounder about in the waves with apparently utter unconsciousness of impropriety'. It was further claimed that respectable families preferring 'a quiet spot' were being driven from the resort by the influx of such types.

During the month of August 1880, 11,410 ordinary and 47,068 excursion passengers arrived in Skegness. The races the following year attracted 25,000 people and, in 1882, the August Bank Holiday passenger figures peaked at 20,000. Because the track was single the last train did not leave Skegness, until 2.30 am on Tuesday, many people spending the night on the streets.

The railway company paid Lord Scarborough a farthing for every excursion ticket purchased to allow ticket holders free entry to the Pleasure Gardens. However, unlike the Manchester, Sheffield & Lincolnshire Railway which spent vast amounts of money developing the resort of Cleethorpes, Skegness received no direct support from the GNR. Lord Scarborough's agent, H.V. Tippet, persuaded the GNR to increase train services, especially from London, and, despite accusations of desecration of the Sabbath, to run trains on Sundays.

On Monday 2nd October, 1932, the first excursion carrying 650 passengers left the nearly completed GNR terminus at Leicester (Belgrave Road), bound for Skegness.

From Leicester (Belgrave Road) trains ran to Marefield North Junction and then over the GNR & LNWR Joint via Melton Mowbray and Harby and Stathern to Redmile and Bottesford South Junction, joining the GNR Nottingham-Grantham line at Bottesford East Junction as far as Allington Junction. Trains continued towards the coast passing under the GNR main line, and, at Barkston East Junction, joined the Grantham-Boston line and on via the East Lincolnshire line to Firsby South Junction.

Prior to the opening of the GNR and Great Central Railway (GCR) joint station at Nottingham (Victoria) in 1900, the GNR ran from the London Road terminus. Excursion trains from Nottingham followed a more direct route than their Leicester counterparts to the seaside. Travelling to Bottesford East Junction via the Nottingham-Grantham line, at which point they followed the route taken by the Leicester trains. Some of the trains travelling from Burton-upon-Trent, Derby (Friargate) and Pinxton avoided Nottingham (Victoria) by taking the line via Daybrook and Gedling to Colwick North Junction and Rectory Junction. Excursions travelling over the Mansfield Railway and calling at Kirkby-in-Ashfield and Mansfield 'Central' joined the former Lancashire, Derbyshire & East Coast Railway (LD&ECR) at Clipstone. This was the link between the LD&ECR route and the GCR main line and provided access to Lincoln and thence to the coast. There were times when LNWR engines on excursions ran right through to Skegness.

The problem of whether the Skegness line should be absorbed by the GNR or a longer lease be negotiated arose in 1894, the working agreement being due to expire in August. In May the GNR Board offered to buy the shares of the company at £15 each. In November terms were agreed at £17 per share for each of the 4,500 £10 shares; the working agreement was extended to December 1895. By an Act of 30th May, the GNR absorbed the Wainfleet company as from 1st July, 1896, at a price of £576,500.

Now that the line was its own the GNR decided to double the track, the powers for which were obtained on 25th July, 1898. Lord Scarborough had agreed to provide land for the enlarging of Skegness station, with the proviso that the work was completed by August 1899. The first estimate for the doubling was for £50,000 but this was amended to £62,477. Work on doubling the line was in progress by May 1899 and had reached Thorpe Culvert by 9th July, Wainfleet soon afterwards and was completed in June 1900, in time for summer traffic. Another island platform was provided at Skegness, the refreshment room improved and an overall roof erected over the concourse.

Skegness continued to enjoy increasing numbers of visitors during the early 1900s, the figures rising from 226,887 in 1902 to 321,260 in 1907. In July 1905 the GNR introduced a dining car in one direction and a breakfast car in the other on the Nottingham-Skegness service. Cheap excursions to provincial, as well as

1424 SATURDAY, 28th JULY.

Gainsboro' and Lincoln to Boston & Skegness and back.—(Workmen's excursion.)

With bookings, Lincoln to Woodhall Spa, Horncastle, Firsby, Spilsby and Sutton Bridge

Down

Station		228 A.M.	229 A.M.	230 ordy A.M.	231 A.M.	Empty coaches P.M.
Gainsboro'	dep.	...	...	...	6 30	
Lincoln { T.P.	arr.	...	...	...	6 55	
Station	dep.	5 10	5 20	6 10	7 0	
Washingboro'	"	5 16	5 26	6 16	7 5 *	
Kirstead	arr.					
Woodhall Spa	"			6 40		8 15
Horncastle	"			7 24		8 37
Boston	"			7 40		
Firsby East Junction	dep.	6 5	6 15	7 10	7 58	
Firsby Stn.	arr.	6 17	6 25		8 10	
Spilsby	"	6 42	6 50	8 57	b 35	
Sutton Bridge	"			9 16		
Skegness	"	6 57	7 5	9 20	8 50	

Up

Station		228 P.M.	231 ordy P.M.	231 P.M.	232 ordy P.M.	232 P.M.
Skegness	dep.	5 35	...	6 0	7 20	...
Sutton Bridge	"	...	5 40	...	7 20	...
Spilsby	"	...	5 46	...	...	...
Firsby Stn.	"	...	6 16	...	6 16	...
Firsby East Junction	pass	6 16	6 52	6 40	spcl. 8 41	...
Boston	arr.	6 16	6 52	6 40	...	9 20
"	dep.	6 28	6 54	...	...	9 32
Horncastle	"	...	...	...	9 17	9 38
Woodhall Spa	"	...	...	...	...	...
Kirkstead	arr.	...	...	...	...	...
Washingboro'	dep.	7 15	7 40	8 20	9 42	9 43
Lincoln { T.P.	arr.	7 20	7 45	...	...	10 4
Station	dep.	7 25	7 50	...	...	10 9
Gainsboro'	arr.	8 20	7 55	...	...	10 13

Specials will probably be run in duplicate.

Mr. Lindsey to provide guards for 231 special. Mr. Reading to provide guards for 228, 229 and 230 specials. Respective station masters to arrange train staff working. 232 to be worked by engine, guard and coaches of 38 Up Loop. Mr. Halliday to arrange.

* 2 up Loop goods to be kept clear.

† Precede 20 up ordinary.

Long-date passengers return by ordinary trains from Sutton Bridge, Spilsby, Skegness, Firsby, Boston, Horncastle and Woodhall Spa on the following Monday, Tuesday or Wednesday.

Long-date passengers holding Lincoln to Skegness tickets may return to Wainfleet or Boston on Saturday night, and remain there until the following Monday, Tuesday or Wednesday, travelling from stations named to Lincoln by any ordinary train. Long-date passengers holding Gainsboro' to Skegness tickets may return to Wainfleet, Boston or Lincoln on Saturday, and remain there until following Monday, Tuesday or Wednesday, travelling from stations named to Gainsboro' by any ordinary train.

Second outward special to run forward to Skegness only if necessary, and be kept clear of 6 down E. L. ordinary.

Horncastle to Kirkstead special to be worked by Boston engine and guard of 13/59, which must run correspondingly later to Boston.

A GNR Special Working Notice for the 28th July, 1900.

GREAT NORTHERN RAILWAY.

Trips to the Lincolnshire Coast.

SWITCHBACK RAILWAY & OTHER ATTRACTIONS AT SKEGNESS.

CHEAP 1, 3 OR 4 DAYS' EXCURSIONS

WILL RUN AS UNDER :

21st July, see separate bill.

TO SKEGNESS.

July 2nd and 11th, 16th and 30th, August 1st, 2nd, 13th and 15th, and September 3rd.

TO SUTTON-ON-SEA AND MABLETHORPE.

July 16th and 30th, August 1st and 13th, and September 3rd.

STATIONS.		July 2nd	July 11th, Aug. 2nd and 15th.	July 16th & 30th, August 13th and Sept. 3rd.	August 1st only.	DAY TRIP.		3 or 4 DAYS.	
		a.m.	a.m.	a.m.	a.m.	s.	d.	s.	d.
MOORGATE ... dep.		...	6 58	6 58	6 23				
Aldersgate ... ... ,,		...	7 0	7 0	6 25				
Farringdon... ... ,,		...	7 2	7 2	6 27				
KING'S CROSS (G.N.) ,.		5 40	7 30	7 40	6 50				
Holloway ... ... ,,		5 35	7 8	7 35	7 15				
Finsbury Park ... ,,		5 45	7 35	7 45	7 20	5	0	6	6
Harringay ... ... ,,		5 34	7 13	7 13	7 1				
Hornsey ... ... ,,		5 36	7 18	7 15	7 3				
Wood Green ... ... ,,		5 39	7 23	7 20	7 5				
New Southgate ... ,,		5 55	7 40	7 50	7 10				
New Barnet ... ... ,,		...	7 50	8 0	7 35				
Skegness ... arr.		8 52	11 5	11 35	10 25				
Sutton-on-Sea ... ,,		...	...	11 50	11 10				
Mablethorpe .... ,,		...	...	11 55	11 15				

DATES AND TIMES. — Fares there and back, Third Class.

RETURNING AS UNDER :

Passengers with day trip tickets issued July 2nd, return same day only from SKEGNESS at 7.0 p.m.

Passengers with day trip tickets issued July 11th, August 2nd and 15th, return same day only from SKEGNESS at 5.50 p.m.

Passengers with day trip tickets issued July 16th and 30th, August 13th, and September 3rd, return same day only from MABLETHORPE at 6.35 p.m., from SUTTON-ON-SEA at 6.45 p.m., and from SKEGNESS at 7.25 p.m.

Passengers with day trip tickets issued Monday, 1st August, return same day only from MABLETHORPE at 6.20 p.m., from SUTTON-ON-SEA at 6.25 p.m., and from SKEGNESS at 6.10 p.m. for Finsbury Park, Holloway, King's Cross, Farringdon, Aldersgate, and Moorgate; and from MABLETHORPE at 6.20 p.m., from SUTTON-ON-SEA at 6.25 p.m., and from SKEGNESS at 6.30 p.m., for New Barnet, New Southgate, Wood Green, Hornsey and Harringay.

Passengers holding 3 or 4 days' tickets issued Mondays return on following Wednesday or Thursday ; those holding similar tickets issued Tuesday return on following Thursday or Friday ; and those holding similar tickets issued Saturdays return on following Monday or Tuesday by any ordinary or special train having a through connection.

For excursion to Skegness on Thursday.

An extract from the GNR's *London Excursion Programme*, 1904.

Above: An early GNR poster of Skegness showing the pier and the delights of steam and sail.

Right: John Hassall, painter of the famous 'Jolly Fisherman' poster used by the GNR to promote excursions to Skegness and still used as a symbol for the resort.

Hassall's follow-up poster to the 'Jolly Fisherman'.

Boston station prior to the upward extension of the water tank brick support. Single No. 221 was built in July 1876, and withdrawn in August 1909. The locomotive was rebuilt in June 1899 but reverted to a straight back boiler in June 1907.   *Lens of Sutton*

GNR 'Large Atlantic' No. 1427 with its passengers, crew and railway staff stands at Skegness station in the early 1900s. No. 1427 was not very old when this photograph was taken having been built in 1907, she was withdrawn in February 1945.   *Winston Kime Collection*

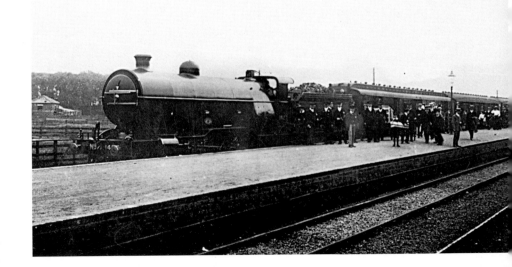

seaside towns, were a developing market for the GNR. Skegness, although popular with the Midland excursionists, had only enjoyed modest success in London. However, in the summer of 1905 day excursions, often on a Sunday, were offered from Kings Cross with great success. On the August Bank Holiday six trains were required to work to Skegness.

On 13th February, 1908, the GNR purchased an oil painting from the artist John Hassall. It depicted a pipe-smoking fisherman skipping along a beach. The GNR added the words 'Skegness is so bracing' and the resulting poster appeared at Kings Cross advertising trips from that station to Skegness for 3s. 6d. return. The poster was a sensation and became one of the most enduring images of seaside holiday advertising. The half-day trips from Kings Cross became legendary. Running on Monday, Thursday and Sunday during July and August the trains were formed of corridor stock and left Kings Cross at 11.30 am taking 3½ hours for the 131 mile trip. They became so popular that, in 1909, it was required to run the Bank Holiday trip in no fewer than 10 portions carrying some 6,000 passengers. The number of trippers at Skegness increased to 356,409 in 1910 and, in 1913 ¾ million people visited the resort. By August 1914 the figure stood at 407,000. Although such enterprise vanished at the outbreak of World War I, a heavy programme of excursion traffic, with trains originating from a multitude of stations, continued to serve the resort year after year.

Joseph Traxler described a cheap day excursion from Kings Cross to Skegness in the early 1900s:

At the time Hassall's 'Jolly Fisherman' adorned the billboards, the trip was one of the 2s. 9d. excursions, this represented a reduction from the original fare. When the family arrived at Kings Cross we found a corridor train, which was a novelty for a cheap day excursion, it was not unduly full. Father and I walked along the platform to see an Ivatt 4-4-0, I think it was number 46, backing out of Gasworks tunnel. I had my first sight of a 'Large Atlantic' at an adjacent platform, she was tremendous, majestic in her apple green livery. The Atlantic and its train left before us, it was an impressive exit, powerful and confident, safety valves blowing off.

Our excursion left at 11.30 am and we made a good climb to Finsbury Park with the moderate load of nine bogie coaches, about 260 tons. The weather was fine and warm and once over the summit at Potter's Bar No. 46 ran fast. we flashed through Hitchin at 70 mph. Father pointed out the Cambridge branch from which emerged a GER 'Intermediate' 2-4-0 with a train of horseboxes, a lovely looking engine in its royal blue livery.

We rumbled over Nene Bridge and stopped at Peterborough for an unscheduled water stop which was effected in a few minutes, making no difference to our timekeeping as we had made good time so far. At Spalding 46 was taken off and, to my surprise, an old Stirling 8 foot 'Single' was backed on to the train. The 'Single' moved off with some slipping. I watched from the window as we bowled along, the great driving wheel revolving steadily and the connecting rod glistening in the sun, soon the train took the curve at Firsby South Junction, on through Wainfleet to reach Skegness in just under three hours from London.

As well as London and the Midlands, excursionists also came from the West Riding of Yorkshire. From the summer of 1904 there was a Saturdays-only

GNR class 'C1' 4-4-2 'Large Atlantic' on a Kings Cross to Skegness special at East Lincoln Junction, Boston on 15th August, 1907. *P.W. Pilcher/NRM*

GNR 'Large Atlantic' No. 301 hurries through Boston with a Kings Cross to Skegness special during Easter 1913. *P.W. Pilcher/NRM*

Leeds train, soon to run also on Sundays. These were timed for use by day excursionists and ordinary holiday makers. Previously the GNR had run few Sunday trains and the first Skegness Sunday excursionists remarked how quiet the main line was.

Because all excursion trains for Skegness were required to reverse at Firsby station the installation of the south curve was deemed essential. The GNR had obtained powers in 1874 but these had lapsed. In 1879 Henry Oakley asked the GNR Directors to reconsider the south curve, reminding them that the branch connected with the ELR to the north, inconveniencing the majority of travellers who came via Boston and the South and West. The estimated cost for the curve was in the region of £5,000. The Board authorised construction and the Board of Trade inspector reported it satisfactory for the operation of trains on 24th May 1881, although it was not authorised by an Act until 18th July of the same year, two months after it had opened. The double-track, 10 chain-radius curve was 20 chains in length and joined the ELR about 800 yards south of Firsby station. An overbridge to the east enabled a level crossing to be abolished. Two new signal boxes were built at South Junction with 20 levers, four of them spare, and at East Junction which also had 20 levers, six of them spare. At the time there were no gates between the up main line and the Skegness line. Road widening at Firsby gave the opportunity to install the double set of crossing gates which folded over each other when closed, an unusual arrangement.

Trains on the Boston to Skegness route not stopping at Firsby station now travelled round the tight south curve avoiding the station. Trains between Grimsby and Skegness had to set back at the station from the up line to the Skegness line as there were no facing points. This meant that the actual turnout facing the train as it set back had no facing point lock, being installed for shunting movements only. This applied to both possible routes giving access to the Skegness line, the crossover up main line to Skegness bay, or the crossover up main to down main. Before World War II trains were cheerfully set back over the unlocked points, usually into the Skegness bay. In due course tests were carried out to scotch or clamp the points. The scotch was not successful so the clamp had to be used. The result of the new practice was that setting back over the main crossover to the down platform became favoured because it was not so far for the man with the clamp to walk as was the alternative route.

The triangle at Firsby was used to turn engines from both Skegness and Mablethorpe. Both places had turntables but they were not capable of turning the larger engines (the table at Skegness was 44 ft 7 in.). During the early British Railways period a turning triangle was installed at Skegness, south of the running line close by the carriage sidings. The turning procedure at Firsby consisted of the engine travelling on the up main line to Firsby South where it was switched to the down main line round the curve to Firsby East. The engine would reverse again on to the single line leading back to the station, either being turned into the bay platform or into the down platform.

Norman Clark remembers going to work at Firsby station:

I was appointed to Firsby as a porter-signalman in 1929, after being passed as qualified by inspector George Johnson at Lincoln. On arrival at Firsby I was welcomed by station master Newton who introduced me to Harold Roberts who was to take me to South box and show me the ropes. Harold was a porter-signalman at the Station box. Porter-signalman was a bit of a hybrid grade and involved four hours' signal box work and four hours' porter's work to make up the eight hour shift. If you did more than four hours in the signal box you were entitled to signalman's pay. At this time Firsby station box opened at 4.10 am with the regular signalman covering until 12.10 pm when he was relieved by the porter-signalman until 3.00 pm. At this point the late turn signalman took over until the line closed after the passage of the last goods from Grimsby. Signalmen at Firsby at this time were Sam Stones and Fred Easter. Firsby had a large staff with four porters, of whom Alf Hewson and Tom Triffit were two; two ticket collectors, I remember Jack Wright doing this job; clerks included Bert Barford, Eric Would and Harry Hobson, foreman was Jack Chapman; Signal and Telegraph men were Johnny Would, Arthur Wilkins and Ben Knight.

Four men lived at the station, Sam Stones near the crossing gates, the others were Jack Chapman, station master Newton and Arthur Elston. Arthur was the pumper and was responsible for the supply of water for the engines.

A legendary figure at Firsby before my time was station master Joe Toplis whose dealings with the public were not always polite. On one occasion a gentleman's hatless head appeared out of a train window as Joe was passing dutifully calling, 'Over the bridge, Skegness, over the bridge . . .'

'Hey, mister, I've lost me 'at?', interrupted the agitated passenger.

'Then keep your ruddy head in - over the bridge, Skegness . . .'

On another occasion Joe was attending the Grimsby train and was about to give the 'right away' to the guard when a lady passenger alighted and asked Joe what time she would arrive in Grimsby. 'Get inside missus, you'll be there nearly as soon as the train', retorted the annoyed official.

The summer season at Skegness provided a number of extra jobs and consequent promotion for railwaymen. Jack Wright moved from Firsby to Skegness as summer foreman. His position as ticket collector at Firsby was taken over by porter Tom Triffit. The South Junction signal box required two men in the summer season usually myself and Len Smith, who came from Aby. Len eventually went to Willoughby and was largely instrumental in forming the British Railwaymen's Travel Club, which had a big membership and organised group travel for BR men on the Continent.

Because of the severity of the south curve at Firsby it was impressed upon us never to stop a long train on the curve except in an emergency, because some engines would not be able to start off again without assistance from a second engine. Once when I was on duty a long train of empty coaches stopped on the curve, although the signals were clear. The driver got down and came to the box, requesting me to send a message for him, which I did, all the time wondering where I would be able to find an engine to assist. I casually asked the driver if he thought he could get started on the curve. 'Leave it to me and *Butler Henderson*', was his reply and he went back to his engine. A word with his fireman, a toot on the whistle and the ex-GCR 'Director' moved off smoothly, accompanied by memorable pyrotechnics.

After leaving Firsby I was appointed to Burgh-le-Marsh, remaining there until 1935. With the coming of the motor car Burgh became a little railhead for Skegness. Many passengers found it more expeditious to travel the six miles from Skegness to Burgh by road than to take the train from Skegness to Firsby and have to wait there for their train.

Chapter Five

The Kirkstead and Little Steeping Railway (The 'New Line')

During the first 10 years of the 20th century the great railway companies were endeavouring to deal with heavy cross-country mineral and holiday traffic. The public was demanding a quicker more efficient service, and, in many cases, companies provided short but important links of railway to replace what had often been circuitous routes, thus enabling rapid through runs to be made between districts hitherto well-nigh isolated.

The major portion of visitors to Skegness came from London and points south of Grantham through Boston. With the intention of popularising the resort and offering better travelling facilities for passengers from Lancashire and the West Riding, several schemes were proposed to link Lincoln directly with Skegness.

In 1879 Lincolnshire experienced a period of depression due to an abnormally wet late summer and autumn which destroyed the harvest. High river levels flooded thousands of acres of low-lying land for months. If that was not enough there was an outbreak of foot and mouth disease. The success of the GNR in Lincolnshire was, to a great extent, dependent upon the success of the harvest. A bad harvest meant there was less produce to carry out of the county, and, as a result, the inhabitants could only afford the barest minimum of imported products such as coal and other necessities, they also travelled less. It was during these periods that the GNR regarded Lincolnshire as more of a liability than an asset.

It was against this background that, in 1884, when the Commons committee approved the Lincoln & Skegness Railway Bill the GNR, who had opposed the Bill, decided to continue its opposition in the Lords, announcing, 'that from its long and painful experience of lines in East Lincolnshire it would not subscribe to, take over, or work the proposed railway'. The Bill was defeated in the Lords.

An Act of 16th September, 1887 was granted to the 'Lincoln, Horncastle, Spilsby & East Coast Railway', to construct a line from Stixwould, with running powers to Lincoln, to Firsby, and including junctions with the Horncastle, Spilsby and Skegness lines. The aim was to lessen the travelling distance to Skegness from Lancashire and the West Riding. This time the GNR was prepared to work the line for 60 per cent of the receipts. Sufficient capital was not raised and the GNR declined to take over the company's powers when abandonment was sought and granted in 1891.

Despite the fact that the GNR considered it had treated Skegness well, in November 1910 the Skegness town council sought a meeting with Oliver Bury asking for better services from Manchester, Birmingham and Leeds. It suggested a Spilsby-Horncastle line and indicated that if the GNR was not sympathetic they would seek help from the Midland Railway. Bury suggested an alternative new line from Kirkstead to Little Steeping and improved services. At this time, in the summer, there was a Leeds train five days a week, including Sundays, Manchester through carriages attached to the Yarmouth train between Retford and Sleaford, and Lincoln trains, reversing at Boston.

This is an interesting set of photographs taken during the construction of the 'New Line'. All were taken at roughly the same place by Harness Rundle. It would appear they are taken near the unclassified road which ran alongside the Horncastle Canal, which was no doubt the cause of the considerable flooding. *Above*: the construction of an embankment temporarily halted by the flood waters. Notice the steam crane. The view below shows a row of contractors wagons and one of the abutments for the bridge over the unclassified road.

Here we see the contractors wagons from a different angle and also a row of GNR four-plank wagons, the nearest of which is numbered 209. *Below.* The final picture shows another view of the flooding, with a huge pile of bricks in the background.

Coningsby Booking Hall, prior to opening.   *The Engineer*

New Bolingbroke station prior to opening.   *The Engineer*

The GNR Board approved a light railway to run from Kirkstead, on the Lincoln-Boston line, to Little Steeping on the ELR, which would avoid the necessity for trains from Manchester, Sheffield and Lincoln having to reverse at Boston. The estimated cost of the new line was £214,204, which included embankments, bridges, culverts, drains, metalling roads and level crossings, houses permanent way, fencing, sidings, junctions, stations, land and buildings.

Plans were sent to the Light Railway Commission on 18th May, 1911, requiring that it approve an order for the construction of the line. The LRC held an enquiry at Boston on 18th July and granted the order, with protective clauses for the County Council and the drainage authority. The order was confirmed on 27th December, with three years given as the limit for the compulsory purchase of any land required. Although the new railway's official title was 'The Kirkstead and Little Steeping Railway' it was universally known as the 'New Line' and this title will be used throughout this book.

It is interesting that the GNR adopted a light railway method for a line which would carry very substantial holiday traffic. Lord Allerton, the Chairman of the GNR, suggested that such a procedure was a cheaper way of obtaining land.

No time was lost in getting work on the Kirkstead-Little Steeping underway, the Engineer was Alexander Ross. A tender from H. Arnold & Son for £93,993, was accepted and the Doncaster firm began construction at both ends of the line simultaneously in March 1912. McKenzie and Holland supplied the signalling equipment; signal boxes were provided at each station and at Coningsby Junction, Spilsby Road Crossing, midway between Midville and Bellwater Junction, where a further box was built. At the opening each box was a block post. By the end of the line's life Bellwater Junction, Woodhall Junction and Tumby Woodside retained this status, with the boxes at New Bolingbroke and Midville switched in only as required. Signal boxes at Coningsby station, Tumby Woodside and Stickney had 25 levers whilst New Bolingbroke and Midville were provided with 30, the extra ones to deal with the extra long sidings at those places. Spilsby Road Crossing had just 7 levers.

All stations Coningsby to Midville were connected to an omnibus telephone circuit, the signal boxes also being able to speak to the next box by the 'block telephone'. The single needle telegraph was not installed. All other stations to Skegness were on a telegraph circuit. Messages for the New Line were transmitted by Lincoln Telegraph office to Coningsby Junction, who passed them on. The code ringing was as follows:

Coningsby Junction	One Long
Coningsby SB and Office	One long, Three Short
Tumby Woodside SB and Office	Four Short
New Bolingbroke SB and Office	Five Short
Stickney SB	One Long, Two Short
Stickney Office	Two Short, One Long
Midville SB and Office	Two Long
Spilsby Road Crossing	Three Short, Pause, Three Short
Bellwater Junction	Two Short

Coningsby Junction box could also connect this circuit to the Train Control (Lincoln) located at Blankney.

More views from before the opening of the 'New Line'. *Top left:* Bridge over Hobhole Drain. *Top right:* Skew bridge over roadway. *Bottom left:* Road overbridge at Stickney. *Bottom right:* Brick bridge over the River Bain.

(All) *The Engineer*

Stations Boston to Skegness were on a telegraph circuit:

Boston (BO), Sibsey (SI), Old Leake (OL), Eastville (EV), Little Steeping (LS), Firsby
South Junction (FS), Firsby Station signal box (FY), Alford (AF), Sutton-on-Sea (SS),
Havenhouse signal box (HA), Skegness signal box (K).
Skegness was also on the Spalding-Boston circuit.

The line was laid double throughout using 85 lb steel rails and was almost 15
miles in length. The railway left the Lincoln-Boston line at Coningsby Junction,
1½ miles south of Kirkstead station, curved slightly south-east and proceeded
on an easterly direction until it joined the ELR at Bellwater Junction, between
Eastville and Little Steeping. No engineering difficulties of any significance
were encountered during the construction of the line; only one house had to be
demolished and a road near Coningsby slightly diverted. Because of the flat
nature of the countryside through which the line passed no formidable
earthworks were necessary. Throughout the whole length of the line there was
no gradient steeper than 1 in 200 and only three such were encountered, one
approaching Coningsby, one to the east of Stickney and the last rising towards
the ELR at Bellwater Junction. Under such conditions curves were also few, the
sharpest being at Coningsby Junction and at Bellwater Junction, both being of
40 chains radius; the remaining three curves were 2 miles in radius.

Almost all the roads were crossed on the level, the exceptions being two
underbridges at Coningsby, crossing main roads, and a bridge carrying the
road over the line at Stickney. In all cases these were constructed of steel girders
on brick abutments. The same method of construction was utilised to bridge the
numerous drains and watercourses prevalent in the Fens. The only exception
was the skew brick-arch bridge over the River Bain at Coningsby, which was
the only bridge needing piling operations to ensure the stability of the
foundations, the abutments of the others being built on a good solid bottom of
clay. Owing to the somewhat treacherous nature of the subsoil adjacent to the
River Bain it was found necessary to put down brushwood to obviate the
possibility of the bank subsiding.

Ample facilities were provided for dealing with local passenger and goods
traffic in addition to the working of through trains. Stations were provided at
Coningsby, a short distance from the junction, Tumby Woodside, New
Bolingbroke, Stickney and Midville. The station buildings were all constructed
of brick with slate roofs, the usual accommodation being provided for
passengers. Platforms were 400 feet in length, more than adequate for local
traffic, and capable of dealing with excursion trains. All were brick built, except
at Coningsby and Midville, where they were of timber construction.

The Engineer on 31st October, 1913 reported:

By means of this railway the traffic between Sheffield and Doncaster districts, in
particular, and Skegness, will be facilitated to no small extent. Hitherto travellers
between these points were, of necessity, compelled to make a long detour via Boston,
involving possibly constant stoppages and changes. This slow and irritating railway
journey has become a thing of the past, for it is now possible, without change of carriage,
for the holidaymaker to turn his back on the smoke and grime of Sheffield and, in a little

New Bolingbroke station prior to opening.   *The Engineer*

Midville station prior to opening.   *The Engineer*

over 2½ hours find himself amid the pure atmosphere of Skegness. Again the journey between Lincoln and Skegness has been reduced to 1 hour 23 minutes on the express service and 1 hour 38 minutes on the ordinary service, whereas hitherto 2½ and 3½ hours have been occupied by trains travelling via Boston.

The line opened for goods on 1st June and passengers on 1st July, 1913. Four local trains ran each way between Lincoln and Skegness in addition to the express service between Sheffield and Skegness. In the beginning a 25 mph speed restriction was imposed by the Board of Trade, but this was later increased to 50 mph, with the exception of the up through line between Coningsby and Coningsby Junction and the down line through the junction at Bellwater where a 20 mph restriction was in effect.

In 1916 the GNR Board decided to lift one 'New Line' track to assist the war effort. The track was to be relayed in France but unfortunately the vessel carrying the rails sank in the English Channel. The singled line was worked by Staff and Ticket. Although holiday traffic was greatly reduced and tourist tickets withdrawn, the daily Lincoln-Skegness service continued throughout the war. The missing track was reinstated and in use again from 10th July, 1923.

Several notices contained in the *LNER Special Working Notices*, of 20th October, 1924, refer specifically to the 'New Line':

When intimation is received by telephone by the SMs at Coningsby, Tumby Woodside, Stickney or Midville from the gateman at any of the public crossings that a traction engine etc. requires to cross the line, the SM concerned must, if necessary to prevent a delay to a train, arrange for the signal box at either of those stations nearest the crossing on the side from which the next train will approach to be switched into circuit.

Rule 118. Leaving gates across the line at level crossings. Referring to General Rule 118 and subsequent notices for gates to be left across the line between trains does not apply during foggy weather or falling snow at level crossings which are not Block Posts, where no fogmen are provided or where the fogmen have not arrived at their posts, nor at signal boxes after the 'Is Line Clear' has been accepted for a train where no fogmen are provided or where the fogmen have not arrived at their posts. The gates may be left across the line at the following crossings:

Tumby Woodside	}
New Bolingbroke	} Between all trains
Midville	}
Spilsby Road	}
Bellwater Junction	Between trains on Sundays from 10.00 am to 10.00 pm.
Little Steeping	When box closed and between trains when box open.

Coningsby Junction. 15 mph speed restriction over the junction for the New Line and 20 mph for Loop line trains.

Class 'D3' 4-4-0 No. 1316 at Radcliffe with a Nottingham to Skegness and Mablethorpe train in 1922. The sandboxes for reverse running were inside the cab of the engine so that sand could be fed to the trailing coupled wheels instead of behind the leading pair. The coupled wheels were given separate splashers, these two features making No. 1316 unique in its class, remaining so until withdrawal in October 1949.

Real Photographs

Chapter Six

Traffic After World War One

With the opening of the Kirkstead-Little Steeping 'New Line' holiday trains approached Skegness from three directions, Boston, Lincoln, and, to a much lesser extent, Grimsby. Most trains from the GNR system worked to the seaside through Boston, these originated from London and the South, Leicester (Belgrave Road) and Derby (Friargate). Derby also provided access for LMS trains from Birmingham, Stafford and Burton-on-Trent. Trains from Kettering and Northampton used the Nene Valley line to Peterborough. From Boston all trains travelled over the ELR to Firsby South and onto the Skegness line. Trains travelling via Lincoln and over the 'New Line' came from the West Riding and the LMS Knottingley and Pontefract line. GCR trains from Manchester and Sheffield travelled via Retford to Lincoln and Skegness. Trains from Chesterfield and from the GCR and Midland stations in Notttinghamshire travelled over the former LD&ECR.

Trains arriving at Skegness via either the Boston or Lincoln routes constituted the vast majority of the traffic. Only two or three trains arrived at the resort from the Grimsby direction along the ELR. These trains originated in Leeds or Bradford, avoiding Doncaster by using this route. At Firsby these trains had to reverse using the top crossover from the up main line to the Skegness line. Returning trains using this route had direct access from the single line off the branch to the down main line via the through road and main crossover.

Edward Borrill described a trip to the seaside in the late 1920s from a more local starting point:

> We went to the seaside at odd times during the summer usually with my mother and my aunts from Halton mill. We went by train from Halton Holgate (Spilsby branch). Mother would go to the little pop hole and get return tickets for Skegness, we would wait for the 9.50 am from Spilsby, this was the connection for the London express. When the train arrived we got into a compartment coach and we were off. Just before we could enter Firsby station we nearly always had to stop to allow a very long goods train to pass on the main line to Grimsby. In this train would be several different sorts of truck we never saw up the Spilsby branch. Our train would move into the station and the porters would open the doors and shout, 'Over the bridge for Skegness'. Crossing the lines by the footbridge I would notice the large water tank on a high building, this supplied water to the station and the water cranes. In the building under the tank was an oil engine that pumped the water up into the tank.
>
> The Skegness train stood on the branch line platform waiting for the 10.20 am express from Grimsby. Once the express had moved off our train would whistle and set off. Just after the first stop on the branch, at Thorpe Culvert, my mother and I would be on our feet looking out of the window for Thorpe Hall, grandmother would be standing outside waving her apron.
>
> We stopped at Wainfleet, Havenhouse and sometimes at Seacroft before we arrived at Skegness.
>
> Coming home on the train we changed again at Firsby, the Spilsby train was usually waiting just past the station signal box and set back into the platform when we arrived.

LNER

AUGUST BANK HOLIDAY

MONDAY, 5th AUGUST

DAY EXCURSION

TO

LINCOLN, WOODHALL SPA HORNCASTLE and SKEGNESS

FROM	Departure Times	Return Fares—Third Class			
		Lincoln	Woodhall Spa	Horn-castle	Skegness
	a.m.	s. d.	s. d.	s. d.	s. d.
MISTERTON	7 28	2 6	4 0	4 6	7 0
GAINSBOROUGH (Lea Rd.)	7 40	2 0	3 6	4 0	6 0
LINCOLN (L.N.E.R.)	8 10	—	2 0	2 6	No Bkgs.
WASHINGBOROUGH	8 16	—	1 6	2 6	4 6
BARDNEY	8 27	—	1 0	1 3	3 6
SOUTHREY	8 32	—	9	1 6	3 6
HORNCASTLE	8 20	—	—	—	2 6
WOODHALL SPA	8 29	—	—	—	2 6
WOODHALL JCN..............	8 41	—	—	—	2 6
CONINGSBY	8 48	—	—	—	2 6
TUMBY WOODSIDE...........	8 53	—	—	—	2 6
NEW BOLINGBROKE........	8 58	—	—	—	2 0
STICKNEY	9 4	—	—	—	2 0
MIDVILLE	9 10	—	—	—	1 6
Skegness .... arr.	9 37				

Returning from SKEGNESS 6-54 p.m.   HORNCASTLE 7-30 p.m.
WOODHALL SPA 7-40 p.m.   LINCOLN 8-30 p.m.

For particulars of bookings Lincoln to Skegness see other bills

" MID-WEEK " 8 or 15 DAYS' CHEAP TICKETS.
BETWEEN—Any two stations (including Irish Port Stations) by any train.
At single fare and a third (plus fractions of 3d.)

OUTWARD.	RETURN.
Tuesdays (at or after 4.0 a.m.)	Following Tuesday or Tuesday week.
Wednesdays	Following Wednesday or Wednesday week.

" WEEK-END " TICKETS.
BETWEEN—Any two stations by any train.
At single fare and a third (plus fractions of 3d.)

OUTWARD.	RETURN.
Fridays, at or after 4.0 a.m.	Following Saturday, Sunday, Monday or Tuesday.
Saturdays	Same day or following Sunday, Monday or Tuesday.
Sundays	Same day or following Monday or Tuesday.

Where through fares are not in operation, Week-end Tickets will be issued upon 48 hours' notice being given at the station from which the journey will be commenced.
Minimum fares : First Class 4/0 ; Third Class 2/6.
For full particulars see special bills.

Tickets can be obtained IN ADVANCE at the Stations, also at Lincoln from Messrs. Eason & Co., 4, Cornhill, and Messrs. Dean and Dawson, Ltd., 321, High Street.

For Conditions of Issue see over.

London, July, 1929.   (No. 2830)   4,000 L.C.

When the train got on to the Spilsby line we seemed to be moving much quicker than at any time during the journey. It wasn't until years later, when I worked on the branch as a platelayer, that I realised that most of the rails were only 21 feet in length thus increasing the 'click' over the joints.

I can remember a church outing to Skegness when we were given a reserved carriage, road transport was just beginning to be a threat and Mr Mitchell, the station master at Halton, rose to the challenge. The coach was shunted off at Firsby and attached to the Skegness train with the same procedure in reverse on the way home.

The LNER *Holiday Handbook* gave an indication of how much Skegness had developed during the early part of the 20th century:

While quiet seaside resorts relying to a large extent on their natural charms have their appeal to many summer holiday-makers, it is undeniable that the vast number of people yearly seek a thorough change combined with plenty of pleasure and recreation. The rapidity with which Skegness has taken its place in the first ranks of popular British seaside towns, and the fact that it continually increases its attractiveness, is largely due to the admirable way that practically the whole town has been planned and developed as a place of entertainment, and to the facilities the railway has provided for enabling people living, not only in Lincolnshire, but also in Leicester, Nottingham and Derby and other parts of the kingdom to obtain easy and speedy access to it. Its seafront with its North, South and Grand Parades, its pier and its broad expanse of sands so firm that motor speed trials are held on them, present throughout the holiday season scenes abounding with gaiety into which every individual among the thousands there seems to enter wholeheartedly. Among the facilities for sports are two 18-hole golf courses, a miniature course, lawn tennis courts, croquet lawns, bowling greens and cricket grounds. In addition to excellent boating and bathing facilities from the beach, there are sea water baths and a new bathing pool 110 yards long and 25 yards wide. Sand yachting is a very popular pastime. The Rock Gardens, the charming Vine Walk and the tastefully laid out Tower Gardens with their miniature lakes and arbours are a delightful retreat for those who wish for an occasional change from the gaiety of the seafront, seclusion is always to be found along the far extending sands and dunes.

When paid holidays became the norm town factories tended to close during the same week and 'Trip Week' specials were operated to the Lincolnshire seaside. Nottingham, Leicester and Derby people favoured Skegness and Mablethorpe whilst Sheffielders went to Cleethorpes, via Sheffield (Victoria). Tourist Tickets were available at reduced fares between early May and late October with a three month validity for the return journey, these tickets being used for travel on normal services. During the summer of 1928 regular half-day excursions were offered to Skegness on Thursdays, Saturdays and Sundays from Leicester (Belgrave Road) costing 5s. Departure was at 11.20 am, returning from Skegness at 8.00 pm, the journey time about 2½ hours.

In the mid-1930s there were several excursions and special trains which ran to the east coast between July and September, these operated frequently and at standard times over the GNR section. The 7.06 from Derby (Friargate) called at Basford and ran via Daybrook and Gedling arriving at Skegness at 10.02 am. The return journey left the seaside at 7.21 pm. A 7.15 am train left Derby (Friargate) and ran via Nottingham (Victoria), returning at 7.30 pm. An 8.05 am departed from Leicester (Belgrave Road) and called at Humberstone, Melton

Class 'C1' 4-4-2 No. 4409 on a Skegness-Kings Cross train coming off the south curve at Firsby in the summer of 1945.   *T.J. Hepburn*

An anonymous ex-GCR class 'B7' 4-6-0 on a return excursion from Skegness approaching No. 57 crossing to the south of South box in the summer of 1947. The train was probably bound for Sheffield or Manchester as at the time all the 'B7s' belonged to either Sheffield or Gorton. Behind the train the lattice four-arm bracket signal is complete with its finials, which were later, for some peculiar reason, hacked off.   *G.H. Brown*

Mowbray and Bottesford arriving at Skegness at 10.50 am, the homeward journey leaving at 7.00 pm.

GCR section trains worked from Leicester (Central), portions for Cleethorpes and Skegness dividing at Lincoln. Half-day excursions ran from Hucknall (Central), Sheffield (Victoria) and Deepcar.

Saturday and Sunday workings to Skegness during the height of the season left Nottingham (Victoria) at 9.45, 9.50, 10.00, 10.10 and 10.20 am. Trains from Leicester (Belgrave Road) ran at 10.00 and 10.30 am, from Ilkeston at 10.05 am, from Pinxton at 10.05 am, from Burton at 10.20 am and from Derby (Friargate) at 11.14 am. Return journeys from Skegness began at 7.15 pm onwards. Most of these trains made non-stop runs except for a stop at Sleaford to take on water for the engine. Signal boxes along the routes were specially opened at places like Netherfield Junction, Radcliffe, Bottesford East Junction, Allington Junction and Leicester (Belgrave Road).

The LNER ran evening excursions from, for example, Lincoln to Skegness for a return fare of 1s. 6d. On any night several trains would be required, the Lincoln public houses would empty and the Skegness ones fill up. The return trip of 45 miles in non-corridor stock was not without its problems, often trains could be observed in transit with several doors open an inch or two. Evening excursions were offered from Nottingham (Victoria) to Skegness for 2s. 6d. fare for the 160 mile return trip. Trains left Nottingham (Victoria) at 4.00 pm and Pinxton at the same time, arriving at Skegness at 6.04 and 6.36 pm respectively. The return journeys left Skegness at 11.02 pm.

The Eastern Belle Pullman Ltd had two trains of first and third class Pullman cars kept at Stratford, for Newmarket race meetings. These were also used for high class Sunday excursions to Cromer, Sheringham, Aldeburgh, Hunstanton, Yarmouth, Lowestoft or Skegness. Speeds were fast, fares low and meals cheap.

The Working Timetable for the summer of 1937 shows the normal winter 3.55 pm from Skegness to Lincoln replaced by a through train from Grimsby running four minutes later from Firsby. There were additional fast trains to Lincoln, including one to Sheffield, which did not stop along the 'New Line'. This also applied to two services from Mablethorpe. On Saturdays two long distance services travelled the 'New Line', leaving Skegness at 3.40 and 3.46 pm and bound for Leicester (Central) and Manchester respectively. The latter travelled via Firsby, where it reversed and a portion from Mablethorpe was attached.

There were a few variations in the down direction. There was one fewer fast train between Lincoln and Skegness but the early return working from Woodhall Junction (Kirkstead) ran through to Skegness, instead of terminating at Firsby. The Grimsby-Lincoln train was balanced by a train from Lincoln to Louth. There was one other long distance arrival at Skegness via the 'New Line' on Saturdays only, a train from Leeds and Bradford which reversed at Firsby to provide a Mablethorpe connection. In the reverse direction the train was routed through Boston.

Charles Bayes describes a trip to Skegness on 7th August, 1939:

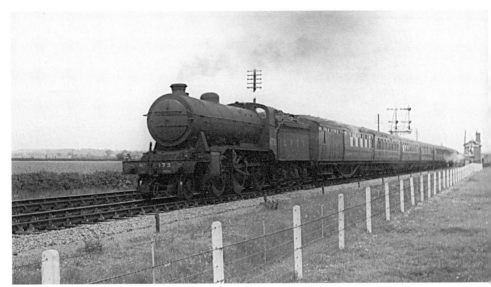

A Colwick-based Class 'K2' 2-6-0 No. 1731 at the South box, Firsby with a train from Skegness on a Saturday in 1947-48. As the engine bears no reporting number it could be a regular summer through train for Nottingham or Derby. With its Gresley coaches this is a train of typical LNER character.   *G.H. Brown*

Colwick-based Class 'K2' No. 1732 on excursion No. 489 at Firsby East with a train from Nottingham or Derby for Skegness. The engine was repainted in post-war green at Cowlairs in October 1947, which would date the photo about spring 1948.   *G.H. Brown*

We had a comfortable journey behind class 'V2' No. 4826 from Kings Cross to Peterborough, a class 'K3' taking over from there. What I had failed to realise was the immense popularity of Skegness with the population of the east and north Midlands. In and around the station in a wide network of sidings were more than two dozen excursion trains and their engines, some already marshalled for their return journeys.

The variety of stock was impressive, LMS class '4F' No. 4420 of Derby Shed headed a 12-coach train and the LNER's own contribution included seven classes of engines and coaches providing every degree of passenger comfort and discomfort. It was the practice to send Kings Cross articulated suburban stock at holiday times to various industrial centres for use on excursions and it was evident that many of them had, as a result, come to Skegness for the day. The destination blinds bore the names of their weekday haunts such as New Barnet and Gordon Hill. An eight-coach train of two articulated sets could seat about 600 people, but leg room and upholstery were minimal. Two trains from Mexborough, each with a class 'K2' in charge were so provided, while a really formidable load of four articulated sets had been hauled from Nottingham by class 'J39' No. 2976. Other trains were more varied in composition and later in the day class 'D9' No. 6040 was seen heading a miscellaneous caravan of 20 vehicles, many of them six-wheelers, to destinations on the M&GN system.

When excursion trains from London to Skegness were formed of suburban stock, they were required to stop at Peterborough on the down journey and at Hitchin on the return trip (all excursions stopped at Spalding in both directions). The extra stops for suburban stock were for examination purposes. This practice continued with British Railways until the coaches were scrapped as diesel and electric trains took over the London suburban services.

Purely local trains to Firsby Junction, some continuing through to Lincoln, had to be fitted in, and class 'D3' No. 4324, 'J6' No. 3074 and 'J39' No. 1896 were employed on these humble duties. Class 'D2' No. 4331 was station pilot and kept very busy. The distant sight of a bright green class 'B4' in the sidings tempted me to trespass beyond the station platforms in order to take a photograph. On my return to the station a couple of policemen were waiting for me, the nature of their suspicion was possible IRA activity. I succeeded in establishing my bona fides but thought it inappropriate to display the packet of railway photos in my pocket taken two months earlier in Cork, Limerick and Dublin!

Engines noted engaged in bringing the thousands of excursionists to the seaside on this last peacetime Bank Holiday were:

'B4' 4-6-0 No. 6104
'D9' 4-4-0 No. 6040
'J6' 0-6-0 Nos. 3543, 3605
'J11' 0-6-0 Nos. 5223, 5246
'J39' 0-6-0 Nos. 1265,1270, 1273, 1276, 1856, 2693, 2704, 2779, 2970, 2976, 2999
'K2' 2-6-0 Nos. 4632, 4635, 4637, 4641, 4643, 4654
'K3' 2-6-0 Nos. 114, 121, 1162

The return journey showed further varieties that had been used on this day. Class 'C2' No. 3259 at Boston and 'B8' No. 5445 at Spalding being the more spectacular examples. We had a punctual return trip to Kings Cross behind class 'V2' No. 4836. A month later War was declared.

During the 1930s peak summer weekends were very busy at Skegness. The August Sunday service would see 40 trains from the south through Boston and west through Lincoln, plus 15 or so via Grimsby in the north. A further half

Class 'K2' 2-6-0 No. 61729 with a train for Skegness on the south curve at Firsby. The single line beyond the engine, to the right, leads into Firsby station. Note also the signalman's cottage beyond the first carriage. *P.H. Wells*

Class 'J6' 0-6-0 No. 64244 leaves Boston with a Skegness excursion on 26th June, 1952. No. 64244 was a Boston-based engine. *Les Perrin*

dozen would be divided between Skegness and Mablethorpe at Firsby. Added to this were the daily services from Lincoln over the Kirkstead & Little Steeping line. Extra sidings were installed at Skegness to help cope with the 100-plus trains a day at the height of the season. All trips would arrive in the morning and have to be dealt with ready for the trip home in the late afternoon or evening.

As the excursion trains arrived at Skegness the incoming crew would be relieved by men supplied by Boston, usually two or three crews and an inspector. It was the relief crew's job to water, coal, oil the locomotive and make sure it was ready to begin its journey home at the appointed time. Each crew would deal with several engines during the day. Two relief foremen involved in this work were driver Bert Hart and driver Ron Barsley. Cyril Clark described weekend working at Skegness:

> These workings were pre-planned on Friday and implemented by the inspectors with the signalmen working under their instructions. On Saturday the signalmen doubled up from 10.30 or 11.00 am until 2.30 or 3.00 pm and there was always a relief signalman assisting with booking, telegraph or the telephone. Firsby station box also had assistance and I was usually booked at one or the other of the boxes from wherever I had been working during the week. On Saturdays during the summer Skegness was a hell-hole. The inspectors had telephone contact with the carriage sidings shunters in order to tell them into which road to place each of the empty trains, and later into which departure platform they should be shunted by the pilot engine ready for the journey home.
>
> Compared with Saturday, when trains were coming and going all the time, Sunday was easier because, apart from branch line trains, most visiting trains arrived in the morning and remained in the sidings until departure in the evening.

The GNR *Appendix to the Book of Rules and Regulations and to the Working Timetables*, dated 1897 and 1912, contain the following instructions with regard to Skegness excursions: 'Guards, brakesmen and others who work as guards or assistant guards of day excursions to Skegness must assist the porters in cleaning out the carriages and must not, without special authority of the station master, leave the station until the carriages are clean'.

If Skegness sidings were full stock would be distributed at sidings along the branch as well as the north sidings at Firsby and on the Spilsby line. The summers in the late 1930s were some of the busiest at Skegness. Certainly after World War II things were never the same again, although during the 1950s and 1960s it was possible to see 40 trains working into the resort on a summer Saturday.

Regular passenger services were withdrawn between Leicester and Peterborough in 1916, to Grantham in 1951 and finally all stations from Leicester (Belgrave Road) to Barnstone and Redmile were closed on 7th December, 1953. The economic survival of the GNR's Leicester branch and the GNR & LNWR joint association had always depended upon goods traffic, Belgrave Road goods depot dealing with local farm produce, boots, shoes and hosiery from local manufacturers as well as incoming traffic.

However, despite the withdrawal of regular passenger services, holiday trains continued to run to Skegness from Belgrave Road at public holidays and

Class 'K3' 2-6-0 No. 61809 of Colwick Shed, at Firsby East Junction with a holiday special for Skegness on 6th September, 1952. *P.H. Wells*

Coming under the East Bridge at Firsby at about 2.30 pm on Saturday 1st August, 1964 is class 'B1' 4-6-0 No. 61031 with a train for Leeds Central. The train will take the line to the station as it is routed via Grimsby and Scunthorpe. *G.H. Brown*

summer Saturdays. The withdrawal of passenger services on several of the routes involved in excursion and special train traffic resulted in several 'half life' stations, which, although closed to regular passenger services, opened for holiday trains. Such places were Pleasly, Skegby and Ashfield Town on the Leen Valley line, which had seen its last passenger services in 1931. By the 1950s the Leen Valley stations saw two trains each way on summer Saturdays, one of which was a Shirebrook North to Skegness working. Although the Lincoln-Shirebrook North service was withdrawn in September 1950 the stations at Shirebrook North, Warsop, Edwinstone and Ollerton remained open for summer Saturday traffic from Basford North to Skegness.

In February 1958 all Eastern Region lines west of Netherfield and Colwick and south of Scalford to London were transferred to Midland Region management. Colwick shed, however, remained an Eastern Region depot. Colwick supplied engines and men working from Belgrave Road, the sub-shed there having closed in 1955. Belgrave Road continued to provide plenty of passengers bound for the seaside during the 1950s. In 1958, 11,867 passengers travelled to the coast in 48 advertised excursion trains.

The following year saw heavy passenger numbers bound for the east coast. During a week in August 1961, Eastern Region carried out a survey of passengers joining or alighting at its stations: 16,000 were recorded at Skegness during the seven days. From June 1963 trains ceased operating from Leicester (Belgrave Road), instead working from Leicester (Central), reversing at Nottingham (Victoria).

From his vantage point at Firsby South Junction Michael Butler observed the finale of seaside steam-hauled excursions:

In the summer of 1962 I saw the 'K3s' and the immaculately turned out No. 61179, chosen by Kings Cross for the final season of the steam-hauled 'Butlins Express'.

In 1963 the Easter Bank Holiday and the summer weekend traffic were the last predominantly entrusted to steam traction. Colwick had 16 'B1s' to call on and with the exception of No. 61336, I noted them all at Firsby South, every one being in commendably clean condition for 1963. Lincoln, Retford, Doncaster, New England, Immingham and Copley Hill examples continued to be employed on regular or extra holiday trains to Skegness and Mablethorpe.

On Saturday 3rd June, 1963 (pre-summer timetable), 23 'B1s' passed Firsby South between 8.15 am and 6.43 pm, 15 going down to Skegness, two on excursions and one light engine, four to Mablethorpe, this included nine Colwick engines; also four on Peterborough-Grimsby workings. On the same Saturday working excursions from the Nottingham area were class '5' Nos. 44658, 44806, 44851 (all 16A), 44690 (15E), 44717 (16D) and 'Crab' No. 42922 (16A), culminating in the last great summer Saturday steam-hauled traffic.

The Ivatt 2-6-0s were not popular choice for working to the coast but three appeared on 27th July, 1963, one on 17th August and Nos. 43066 and 43068 together with no less than 10 Colwick 'B1s' on 24th August.

Further diesel gains in 1964 reduced the summer holiday steam scene to Colwick's 10 'B1s', plus a rather unexpected sight coming from the Grimsby direction. This was the re-routed Leeds-Skegness and, for the few weeks it operated, Copley Hill had been given No. 61031 *Reedbuck*. It was 18 months since a Works visit, but this did not stop the Copley Hill cleaners preparing it to near immaculate standard; by November it had been condemned.

Steam virtually disappeared through Firsby in 1965, a few Immingham engines and the regular weekday Colwick 'B1', heading for Mablethorpe in the summer. However, diesel replacement by steam still happened that summer, Holbeck's Nos. 44828 (3rd July) and 44824 (4th September) substituting for Brush Type '4s' on the Leeds-Skegness; Nos. 61188 and 61127 on consecutive July Saturdays to Mablethorpe and Crewe South's No. 45128 with an extra on 17th July.

Class 'B1' No. 61227 with the 1.18 pm from Skegness to Leicester (Belgrave Road), passing the South box at Firsby. The tail of the train can be seen round the curve, also a good view of the South down home signal.   *G.H. Brown*

Chapter Seven

Local Traffic

Prior to the doubling of the branch in 1900 the Skegness line timetable was as follows:

			Firsby	Wainfleet	Skegness	
			am	*am*	*am*	
5.35	am	Boston LE	6.00	6.11	-	
6.16	am	Wainfleet	-	6.16	6.27	
7.20	am	Firsby 'Mixed'	7.20	-	7.50	
9.05	am	Firsby	9.05		9.29	
11.15	am	Firsby 'Mixed'	11.15		11.46	
11.59	am	Firsby	11.59		12.50	
			pm	*pm*	*pm*	
12.52	pm	Firsby	12.52		1.15	
4.20	pm	Firsby	4.20		4.44	
6.10	pm	Firsby	6.10	6.20	-	Fridays only
7.02	pm	Firsby	7.02		7.25	

			Skegness	Wainfleet	Firsby	
			am	*am*	*am*	
6.35	am	Skegness	6.35		6.59	
8.20	am	Skegness	8.20		8.43	
		To Boston LE	-	9.45	-	Mondays only
		To Firsby LE	-	11.00	11.10	Mondays excepted
9.45	am	Skegness	9.45		10.08	
			pm	*pm*	*pm*	
12.17	pm	Skegness	12.17		12.40	
		Goods to Boston	1.50		-	
3.15	pm	Skegness 'Mixed'	3.15		3.46	
5.40	pm	Skegness	5.40		6.04	
6.35	pm	Wainfleet	-	6.35	6.45	Fridays only
7.35	pm	Skegness	7.35	7.46	-	To Wainfleet only

When Wainfleet shed was operational two engines were stationed there. In the early days the working of Wainfleet engines was confined to Skegness-Firsby branch workings. This later extended to include some trips to Boston, and eventually included trips to Nottingham and Leicester.

During the 1870s 2-2-2 tank engines were shedded at Wainfleet. These were Sturrock conversions of the old Sharp 2-2-2 Singles. They became known as 'boxers' because of their oscillating characteristics. The engines would be sent to Boston for boiler washouts. Small Hawthorn 2-2-2s Nos. 67 and 70 were rebuilt by Stirling and were at Wainfleet during the 1890s. No. 67 was withdrawn in 1900, No. 70 surviving until January 1901.

Hawthorn 0-4-2 goods engine No. 110A, provided with an 'over all' cab and a tender weatherboard, worked the branch in the 1890s. Many of Stirling's 6 ft 6 in. 2-4-0 passenger engines finished their days in Lincolnshire, Boston engines

Shedded at Boston in 1923, class 'E1' 2-4-0 No. 999 is likely to have worked the Skegness branch; seen here at Hitchin in October 1902.   *LCGB/Ken Nunn Collection*

Class '126' 0-4-2 well tank No. 122A as rebuilt with a 4 ft 5 in. diameter Ivatt domed boiler, seen here at Spilsby during World War I. The engine worked both the Spilsby and the Skegness branches.   *Author's Collection*

SKEGNESS BRANCH.

SINGLE LINE—FIRSBY TO FIRSBY EAST, WAINFLEET TO SKEGNESS.—TRAIN STAFF STATIONS—FIRSBY STATION, FIRSBY EAST JUNCTION, WAINFLEET AND SKEGNESS.

Miles from Firsby.	DOWN.	1 Lgh Eng.	2 Pass.	3 Mxd	4 Pas.	8 Mxd		10 Gds.	11 Pas.	15 Ps.	16 Pas. B	18 Pas. A
	From	Boston, train 3, page 115.										
		a.m.	a.m.	a.m.	a.m.	a.m.		a.m.	p.m.	p.m.	p.m.	p.m.
...	**FIRSBY** ......dep.	6 2	...	7 20	9 5	1115	...	11 40	12 52	4 20	6 10	7 2
...	*Firsby east junction* „	...	...	...	...	...	...	..	...	...	..	...
2½	Thorpe culvert ...... „	...	...	7 29	9 11	1124	...	X	12 57	4 25	*	7 7
4½	**WAINFLEET** arr.	6 11	...	7 34	9 16	1129	8 up ...	12 10	1 2	4 30	6 20	7 12
	WAINFLEET dep.	—	6 16	7 35	9 17	1131	...	12 32	1 3	4 32	—	7 14
6	Croftbank .... „	...	*	*	*	*	..	X	*	*	...	*
8	Cowbank .... „	...	*	*	*	*	...	X	*	*		*
9½	**SKEGNESS** ......arr.	...	6 27	7 50	9 29	11 46	...	12 50	1 15	4 44	...	7 25

Miles from Skegness.	UP.	1 Pas. A	2 Pas.	3 Lt.Eng Mons. only.	4 Pas.	6 Lgt. Eng.	8 Pass.		10 Goods	13 Mx.	16 Pas.	17 Ps. B	20 Pas.
		a.m	a.m.	a.m.	a.m	a.m.	p.m.		p.m.	p.m.	p.m	p.m	p.m.
..	**SKEGNESS** ......dep.	6 35	8 20	...	9 35	Mons except'd	12 17	...	1 50	3 15	5 40	...	7 35
1¼	Cowbank .... „	*	*	...	*		*	...	X	*	*	...	*
3¼	Croftbank .... „	*	*	...	*		*	...	X	*	*	...	*
5	**WAINFLEET** arr.	6 47	8 31	...	9 46		1228	10 dn. ...	2 20	3 30	5 52	...	7 45
	WAINFLEET dep.	6 49	8 33	9 35	9 47	11 0	1230	...	3 0	3 32	5 53	6 35	—
6¾	Thorpe culvert .... „	6 54	8 38	...	9 52	...	1235	...	...	3 38	5 58	*	...
...	*Firsby east junc.* ...... „	...	...	...	...	...	...	...	...	...	...	...	...
9¼	**FIRSBY** .... arr.	6 59	8 43	9 45	9 58	11 10	12 40	...	3 10	3 46	6 4	6 45	...
	To			Boston, train 5, page 116.					Boston, train 15, page 116.				

When Firsby east junction is open, all trains and engines must stop at that point to take up or leave train staff or ticket. **A** May take cattle if wagons are fitted with brake pipes. **B** Fridays only.

GNR Working Timetable, 1st October, 1899 for the Skegness branch.

LNER timetable 22nd September, 1930-30th April, 1931 for the 'New Line'.

Table 9 WOODHALL JUNCTION, LITTLE STEEPING AND FIRSBY (via CONINGSBY).

WEEKDAYS.

		Through Train—Lincoln to Skegness.	Through Train—Lincoln to Firsby (SX), Skegness (SO).	Through Train—Lincoln to Skegness.	Through Train—Lincoln to Skegness.
	a.m.	a.m.	a.m.	p.m.	p.m.
Lincoln (L.N.E.) ......dep.	7 55	9 15	1120	4 15	6 0
WOODHALL JUNCTION dep.	**8 47**	**9 41**	**1147**	**4 50**	**6 29**
Coningsby.............. „	8 54	9 48	1154	4 57	6 36
Tumby Woodside .... „	8 59	..	1159	5 2	6 41
New Bolingbroke .... „	9 4	9 56	12 4	5 7	6 46
Stickney.............. „	9 9	10 1	12 9	5 12	6 51
Midville.............. „	9 14	.....	1214	5 17	6 56
Little Steeping.......... „	9 22	..	1222	5 25	7 4
FIRSBY..............arr.	**9 27**	**1014**	**1227**	**5 30**	**7 9**
Firsby..............dep.	10 22	1022	1A30	5 41	7 22
Skegness ....arr.	10 40	1040	1A52	6 2	7 42

WEEKDAYS.

		Through Train—Skegness to Lincoln.	Through Train—Skegness to Lincoln.	Through Train — Firsby to Lincoln.	Through Train—Skegness to Lincoln.
	a.m.	a.m.	p.m.	p.m.	p.m.
Skegness ....dep.	6 35	8 0	1250	3 20	6 20
Firsby..............arr.	6 58	8 23	1 8	3 43	6 38
FIRSBY..............dep.	**7 25**	**8 40**	**1 27**	**4 27**	**6 50**
Little Steeping.......... „	7 30	8 45	.....	4 32	6 55
Midville.............. „	7 38	8 53	1 38	4 40	7 4
Stickney.............. „	7 43	8 58	1 43	4 45	7 10
New Bolingbroke .... „	7 48	9 3	1 48	4 50	7 16
Tumby Woodside .... „	7 53	9 8	.....	4 55	7 24
Coningsby.............. „	7 58	9 13	1 56	5 0	7 29
WOODHALL JUNCTION arr.	**8 5**	**9 20**	**2 3**	**5 7**	**7 36**
Lincoln (L.N.E.) ....arr.	9 7	9 59	2 32	5 35	8 3

A On Saturdays leaves Firsby 12.55 and arrives Skegness 1.13 p.m.

Class 'F2' 0-4-2 No. 110 worked the Skegness and Spilsby lines and was shedded at Boston in 1905 and 1912. Built in October 1885 she was withdrawn in 1921. Seen here at Spilsby.
Author's Collection

Class 'E1' 2-4-0 No. 994 was a Boston engine in 1923 and worked the Skegness branch. Built in 1894 No. 994 was given a 4 ft 5 in. domed boiler in November 1908 and was withdrawn in August 1924. *LCGB/Ken Nunn Collection*

being used on Skegness duties after World War I. Thirty-four class 'E1s' remained in service on 1st January, 1923, of which Nos. 753/5/8, 885, 994/5/8/9, 1061/4/8 were at Boston.

Stirling's '126' class 0-4-2 well tanks Nos. 118A and 122A (later class 'F6') were at Boston in 1908, it is known that No. 122A worked the Spilsby line and equally likely that it, or its partner worked the Skegness branch. Both were withdrawn at Boston in 1918. Class '120' 0-4-4 Back Tanks Nos. 248, 515 and 530A were shedded at Boston, from where they were withdrawn between 1919 and 1921. They saw service on the Spilsby and Skegness branches. The '629' class Back Tank No. 630 was sent to Boston in 1901, condemned by 1905, but reinstated after a heavy repair at Doncaster in 1906. After a spell on the Wansford branches between 1915-17 it returned to Boston from where it was withdrawn in November 1918. Class 'G1' 0-4-4T No. 943 was used on branch line work and withdrawn at Boston in 1924. With the doubling of the Skegness branch locomotive types on the line became more varied. Class 'D3' 4-4-0 Nos. 4358/9 and 4360 were shedded at Wainfleet during the 1930s, for instance. All three engines retained their small boilers and Nos. 4358 and 4360 were attached to Stirling tenders, distinguished by their curved top frame slots, wooden rear buffers and three coal rails. They remained at Boston from 1912 until withdrawn in 1937 and 1935 respectively.

Wainfleet shed diagrams for 1924 showed Engine No. 1 with the first set of men running light to Skegness from where it worked the 7.10 am to Firsby. It continued to work the branch until the 7.28 pm arrival in Skegness station, after which it returned light to Wainfleet. A second set of men who had relieved the first set at 1.35 pm, disposed of the engine before travelling as passengers to Firsby to relieve a Boston crew at 8.45 pm on the changeover engine, which took the 9.15 to Skegness and the 10.15 pm back to Wainfleet.

Engine No. 2 ran light to Skegness at 6.50 am to work the 7.25 am through coaches to Nottingham as far as Firsby, where they joined the 7.10 am Mablethorpe to Nottingham service. The Wainfleet engine then took the 8.40 am Firsby to Lincoln passenger train returning with the 11.20 am to Firsby. The exception was Mondays when an engine ran light to Firsby to work the 8.40 am. Wainfleet men did not go to Lincoln, they changed with Lincoln men who had worked the 5.15 am goods from Lincoln to Firsby with a Lincoln engine. On arrival at Lincoln the Lincoln crew was relieved by a second set of men who took the 11.20 am back to Firsby. Here they changed footplates with Wainfleet men, the Lincoln crew and engine returning home with the 1.32 pm goods. At 12.38 pm Wainfleet men took the engine light up the ELR to Willoughby for the 1.10 pm to Louth via Mablethorpe passenger train, returning light to Firsby. Wainfleet men changed here with Boston men who took the 3.55 pm to Lincoln, afterwards working back to Boston via the Loop line, the Wainfleet men returning home as passengers. Additionally, Wainfleet men worked a local goods train to Alford departing Firsby at 11.52 am and returning on the 1.20 pm pick-up goods to Boston as far as Firsby, using a Boston engine.

A Lincoln engine had worked the first down train to Skegness, returning from there at 12.50 pm. Retford shed was responsible for the third down working and the final up train to Lincoln. After working from Boston via the

Class 'D3' 4-4-0 No. 4304 stands at Firsby station in 1934. Next to the engine is the early station nameboard which proclaims, 'Firsby - Junction for Wainfleet, Skegness and Spilsby'. This was eventually replaced by a BR tin sign with the legend 'Firsby', around 1957.   *J.E. Kite*

Ex-GNR class 'D3' 4-4-0 No 4359, seen here at Boston on 2nd July, 1936, was a Wainfleet engine during this period.   *H.C. Casserley*

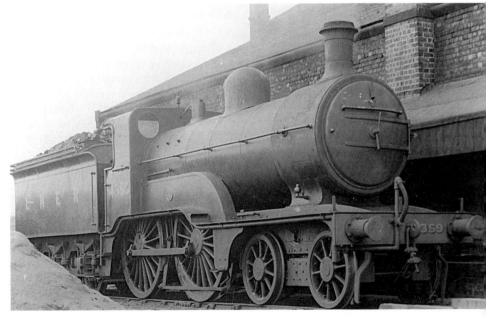

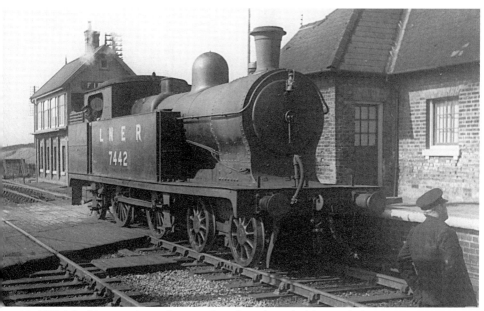

No. 7442 is backing onto its coaches, seen here from the end of the up platform. Harold Penson stands in the 6 foot in earnest conversation with someone on the platform. The date is March 1948 and No. 7442 is an ex-GCR class 'C14' 4-4-2, built by Beyer, Peacock in 1907 and withdrawn in November 1957. *G.H. Brown*

Class 'J11' 0-6-0 No. 4305 at the down platform Firsby station, *c.* 1947. It has just come from, or is just about to depart for, Skegness as the main crossover is set. *G.H. Brown*

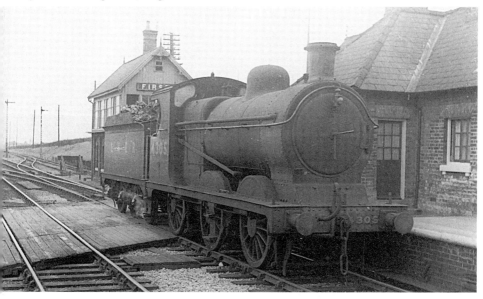

The star of this photograph must be the superb lattice post somersault signal, seen here with its finial. The engine is an ex-GCR class 'C4' 4-4-2 No. 2910, seen here with a 'New Line' goods train in the spring of 1948; No. 2910 was withdrawn the following year. *G.H. Brown*

Messrs Dickson and Duncan loading mail onto a Skegness local in late 1947, in the Skegness branch platform at Firsby station. The small roofboard above the heads of the onlookers reads 'Skegness'. *G.H. Brown*

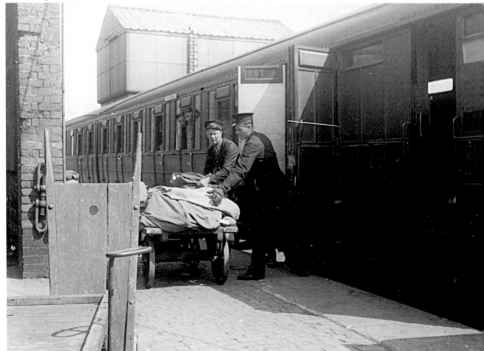

Loop a Boston engine covered the last down train, ending its day at Wainfleet and replacing the engine which had returned to Boston earlier.

Mr R. Hudson described the daily engine changeover procedure at Wainfleet shed during the 1930s: 'Boston men worked the service on the 'New Line'. One of the turns was Boston to Woodhall Junction,* then across the 'New Line' to Skegness. At Skegness we changed engines with Wainfleet men. They had a new engine, we took their engine back to Boston for washing out. Wainfleet had no engine of its own during and after World War II, it came under Boston.'

At Wainfleet there were three sets of drivers and firemen who worked a roster. Two sets worked the passenger service from Skegness to Firsby, meeting the main line trains. The other set worked the afternoon goods to Boston, picking up at Little Steeping, Eastville and Sibsey (on the ELR). This train conveyed potatoes and beet for Spalding and other farm produce which was remarshalled at Boston and worked to various destinations in the evening, the 8.25 to London, 8.30 to Doncaster and the 10.30 pm to Peterborough, as well as a train to Ardsley.

By the 1950s engines supplied by Boston to work the branch were mostly class 'J39' 0-6-0, class 'J6' 0-6-0s (No. 64247 was one), ex-GCR tank engines, class 'A5' 4-6-2s (Nos. 69808 and 69805), and later the British Railways Standard class '4MTs'. Two goods trains left Boston for Skegness every weekday, at 5.00 am and 6.05 am. The first delivered coal to the gasworks at Skegness and would work the first passenger train to Firsby and back, after which it shunted the yard at Skegness. The second engine returned to Boston with the afternoon pick-up goods. The early morning goods would include a van of Mackeson stout delivered to Wainfleet, the home of Bateman's brewery. This had arrived at Boston by train No. 366 which left West Yard, New England, at 1.50 am.

Algy Epton recalled,

I do not know how long we had to wait at Skegness before departure with the return working of the early morning goods, but I recall Jim Walker and I walking along the seafront quite absorbed in the lovely morning when we realised that it was only five minutes to departure time. The engine was No. 64247 (class 'J6' 0-6-0) freshly outshopped from Doncaster works. As we approached Havenhouse station platelayers were working, they had not heard us approaching and left the jack under the rail in their haste. We were pretty nearly tipped off the rails and were very shaken by the experience.

In the 1930s the afternoon return goods to Boston left Skegness at about 3.30 pm and travelled via the south curve at Firsby. This required the signalman, after his midday shift in the station box to walk to the South Junction box and open it for the passage of the goods train. This arrangement continued until the end. There were three up and three down passenger trains between Skegness and Lincoln daily. The first through train left Skegness at 7.55 am, arriving in Lincoln at 10.08 am. Up trains would reverse at Firsby where, very often, a van of fish or perishable goods was attached. The last passenger train to arrive at Skegness was the 6.37 pm ex-Lincoln which was crewed by men off the 4.25 pm Boston to Lincoln service. The crew always had their 'snap' up in the signal box prior to leaving light engine for Boston (signalmen at Skegness in the 1940s and

* Kirkstead was renamed Woodhall Junction in 1922.

Class 'J6' 0-6-0 No. 64190 in very clean condition at Boston on 23rd June, 1958. Designed by Gresley, and introduced in 1911 this class of engine was very familiar in Lincolnshire, both on local workings, as well as bringing excursion trains from the Midlands. Despite its pristine condition No. 64190 was scrapped at Doncaster just over a year later.   *R.C. Riley*

An ex-GCR Class 'J11' 0-6-0 No. 64346 takes the Lincoln to Firsby pick-up goods out of Tumby Woodside station on 19th July, 1961. The signal box and station house are typical of the style throughout the line.   *D.B. Swale*

1950s were Alf Knowles, who was NUR Branch Secretary, and Albert Naylor). All of these trains, except the last passenger train from Skegness, either originated in or terminated at Sheffield by means of a through service or a branch connection.

H.A. Bloy worked troop trains to and from Skegness during World War II. Butlin's Holiday Camp had been commandeered by the navy and became HMS 'Royal Arthur' for the training of navy personnel:

> I can remember working tender first over the Skegness branch in the early morning. A German plane had a pop at us, the driver and I sheltered behind the coal bunker, all the time travelling towards Skegness station. Fortunately we were not hit and were able to approach the terminus as usual.
>
> On another occasion at night, on the Wainfleet-Skegness section, a bomb was dropped in a field close enough to the railway for us to feel the blast. At this time the Railway Authority would not allow any locomotive to remain overnight in the vicinity of what was designated 'invasion coast'. Wainfleet and Spilsby engines went to Boston and from there with the Boston engines in four convoys to Sleaford. They remained there for the night and returned to their places of work early the next morning.

Drivers based at Wainfleet included Messrs Sutton, West, Robinson, Cross and Barwick; firemen were Myers, Allsworth, Leary, Jim Walker and George Walker. Jim Walker, who was there in 1948, recalled 'Sluffy' Barwick:

> He was quite a character, very small so that his top coat touched the ground, his pockets were always filled with rags. He used to pinch your tea and eat all your food. Although he was not very big, when he got his shoulder under the regulator you went like hell, he was as mad as a hatter. The engines we had at this time were GCR tank engines (class 'A5'). We had three guards, one of whom was called Bill Neal; 'Sharp

Boston Loco in 1952, *left to right*, Boston station shunter Bill Ibott, driver Bert Hart, who was one of the relief foremen at Skegness during the summer period and Algy Epton, a young fireman who worked the Skegness branch and helped with this book.

Author's Collection

Ancient and modern meet at Lincoln Central in January 1955. The first diesel unit to arrive at Lincoln *en route* for Skegness. The steam locomotive is class 'B1' No. 61248 *Geoffrey Gibbs*.

P. Grey

A brand new dmu runs into Firsby station from the north with a service to Skegness on 30th July, 1955. *B.N. Collins*

pencil Bill', he was always taking his watch out of his pocket, so much so that he eventually wore a hole in it. If you asked him the time he never knew it but he would book you if you were half a minute late. The other guards were called Tommy Bartram and a chap named Cox.

In about 1950 Wainfleet became a depot on its own, this was when rest days first started. I think we had a day off every three weeks, all passed firemen covered the drivers who were off and the firemen were covered from Boston. [This arrangement remained until the advent of dieselisation in 1955.]

During the 1950s crews stationed at Wainfleet were driver Jack Cross with his fireman Jim Walker, driver Nelson Robinson with fireman Don Leary and driver Barwick with his fireman George Walker. Both Jim Walker and Don Leary were passed for driving and acted in that capacity when their rostered drivers were off, possibly George Walker was also passed for driving. Barwick had worked on the Spilsby branch until its closure to passengers in 1939 at which point he returned to Boston depot. He travelled from Spilsby to Boston and back daily, a journey of some 18 miles each way, on a bicycle fitted with a cyclemaster motorised unit fitted to the rear wheel. No doubt this arrangement continued when he was transferred to Wainfleet.

On summer Saturdays in the late 1940s and 1950s Boston men worked three trains to Kings Cross just after nine in the morning. The first one returned with the 12.18 pm Kings Cross to Skegness. The second came back on the 2.18 pm with the third coupled to it as far as Boston where it came off and went on shed. In the early 1950s a train left Nottingham with 12 carriages every weekday, the engine and six carriages went to Skegness, the remaining six were taken to Mablethorpe by Boston men. A Boston fireman, usually a passed cleaner, would travel with the Skegness portion of the train, usually a class 'K3' 2-6-0 in charge which would be kept adjacent to the coal stack in the loco road on the triangle. The fireman's duties were to clean the fire, coal the tender and fill the water tank. The Nottingham men, usually from Colwick, were booked off, until the return working at 6.10 pm.

A Skegness to Lincoln dmu entering Tumby Woodside station in May 1963. Notice the booking hall on the left, the two elegant somersault signals and the row of railway cottages on the right.   *Mike Black*

With the closure of Wainfleet shed men were still stationed at Wainfleet but Boston men would take an engine to Skegness in the morning and work the first train to Firsby where they would be relieved by Wainfleet men, who then worked the branch. At this time the branch carriages were returned to Wainfleet each night; a guard, Mr Sheard, was stationed at Wainfleet and he would travel with the train to Skegness in the morning to begin the service on the branch.

Diesel traction was introduced into Lincolnshire on Monday 25th April, 1955. With the beginning of the Summer Timetable on Monday, 13th June, lightweight diesel units were introduced on a large number of local services in Lincolnshire. One such was a Lincoln to Skegness service which was used as a connecting service for passengers travelling from Sheffield and intermediate stations. Many of the services between Lincoln and Skegness were replaced and an additional Skegness to Lincoln service at 7.22 pm was brought into operation.

Two new services were announced to run, Saturdays excepted, at 1.37 pm Skegness to Firsby and 2.00 pm from Firsby to Skegness. Sunday services included several new Boston-Skegness connections with non-stop trains, Boston to Skegness at 9.15 am and 8.12 pm and in reverse at 11.30 am and 12.20 pm. Among additional steam driven trains was a new service from Kings Cross to Skegness running at 11.48 am, on Saturdays only, until 3rd September.

By 1959, the Skegness branch was being operated by dmus; rural services, including the 'New Line', followed and when Boston Motive Power Depot closed in 1964 there were five diesel sets stationed there.

In the 1980s Peterborough men worked to Skegness on Sundays. They booked on duty at 9.16 am and worked to the seaside where they took an intermediate rest before working back to Peterborough. The working was altered in 1981 to a single man working.

The 1981 changes coincided with the use of dmus on the service, three or four sets usually making up the train. Prior to this a class '37' English Electric had been used. The advantage of the dmus was that they could remain in the arrival platform until departure, the porters cleaning the train in the meantime. There was also a saving in that a shunter was no longer required to run the locomotive round its train.

Algy Epton recalled:

> The first week the dmus operated the service the driver on the return working to Peterborough was filling radiators with water at Boston, Sleaford and Grantham. The second week, 28th June 1981, I was the driver on the 2.55 pm turn. I had arranged with my train crew supervisor that on return to Peterborough at 8.17 pm I could go home as had arranged to go to a dance. The supervisor was doubtful whether I would make it as the driver had not got back until 10.00 pm the previous week. However, he agreed that if I got back at the booked time I could go.
>
> When I arrived at Skegness I took a watering can and filled up all the radiators on the train, although it was not the driver's duty I felt I was helping myself. The return journey was trouble free and I got home, showered, changed and was at the dance by 9 o'clock.
>
> Being a former Boston man the route knowledge gained from my firing days meant that I was often used on this route, working both turns between 1980 and 1985 ten times. This train although initially well patronised, ceased to run after the summer of 1985, due to lack of viability.

Chapter Eight

The Stations and their Work

The 'New Line'

The extensive coverage of Stickney station in this section is due to notes provided by Derek Fox, and, although particular to that place, describes many events and day-to-day happenings familiar to Lincolnshire country stations in general. The majority of the staff mentioned by name were working during the period 1935-70.

With the formation of Coningsby Junction, which joined the 'New Line' to the Boston-Lincoln line, a new signal box was built in 1912 and equipped with 35 levers. The frame was replaced by a 25-lever Saxby & Farmer 5 in. rocker frame in 1917, which remained in service throughout the life of the box. When the Boston-Lincoln line closed in 1963 the points were clamped. Coningsby Junction signal box closed on 13th July, 1964. Coningsby Junction signal box came under the control of Woodhall Junction station. 'Old man' Giles was in charge of the Junction box, when he retired he was replaced by Ted Wright, from Donington-on-Bain. Other signalmen were Fred Andrews, who later went to Sleaford West, and C. Osgodby.

Prior to the opening of the 'New Line' the occupation crossing on the East Lincolnshire Railway near what became Bellwater Junction, was controlled by a four-lever ground frame sited alongside a crossing keeper's hut. The new signal box was built to control the junction of the New Line with the East Lincolnshire line. The box was supplied with a 25-lever Saxby & Farmer 5 in. rocker frame. The box at Bellwater Junction survived the closure of the New Line and still stands, reduced to little more than the status of a rather grand crossing keeper's hut.

The signal boxes at Coningsby Junction and Bellwater Junction opened at 6.30 am, the rest at stations in between opened at 7.30 am, remaining open until 7.00 pm in the winter, after the passage of the last passenger train, the 6.00 pm from Lincoln to Skegness. In the summer the last train was the 7.30 pm from Skegness to Lincoln and all boxes and crossings remained open accordingly. All boxes were opened for the passing of Saturday summer trains and the Sunday specials to Skegness. In mid-summer, on Wednesdays and Thursdays, the boxes remained open beyond 7.00 pm for the passage of trains travelling to Lincoln over the 'New Line'.

Coningsby

A large village on the banks of the River Bain, two miles north of the River Witham and originally served by Dogdyke station on the Boston-Lincoln line. The most prominent feature in the village is the 15th century grey stone church clock tower with its huge 16½ feet-diameter clock face and single hour hand. Lawrence Eusden, perhaps the least distinguished Poet Laureate ever, was

Coningsby station in August 1970, looking east towards Tumby Woodside. Here, as at Midville, the platforms were of wooden construction.   *P. Grey*

Coningsby station looking west towards Coningsby Junction, in August 1970.   *P. Grey*

rector here, his 'Ode to King George II' a perfect example of his ineptitude; 'Thy virtues shine peculiarly nice, Ungloomed with confinity to vice'.

After leaving the Boston-Lincoln line at Coningsby Junction, (a meeting of the oldest, the Boston-Lincoln, Lincolnshire Loop line) and the newest (the 'New Line''), of the GNR system in Lincolnshire), the line crossed two level crossings, a road underbridge, the River Bain and entered Coningsby station via a bridge over the B153 road. The station was situated on an embankment. There were parallel wooden platforms with single-storey brick-built waiting shelters with shallow hipped roofs. A wooden canopy spanned the length of each building. A single-storey red brick booking office stood at the west end of the down platform. The station master's house and weighbridge office were of the standard pattern for the line.

A signal box, which was taller than others along the line, was situated to the east of the up platform, opposite a siding and goods yard. Most of the original GNR signals here were later replaced by LNER upper quadrants. The up starting signal also carried a lower distant arm which worked in conjunction with the signal protecting the level crossing over a minor road west of the station.

Porter-signalmen at Coningsby were Jack Bass and Dick Allinson. Their times were 7.30 am to 3.00 pm, and 11.30 am to 7.00 pm. Station master during World War II was Mr A. Allcock, the last man-in-charge was Don Loft. Other staff were porter Alf Ball and clerks Sheila Creasey and Winnie Cooper; Bert Usher drove the railway lorry. Signal fitter Capindale was assisted by a man called Boothby. Permanent Way ganger Harry Brant lined his staff up on the platform with their bicycles at the end of the working day. When he blew his whistle at 4.30 pm they could move off! Relief crossing keeper C. Rushier covered all the local crossings for several years.

During World War II Coningsby took deliveries from munition trains several times a week. These consisted of considerable amounts of bombs and ammunition for the nearby RAF station. Many of the bombs were stored on the grass verges of lanes in the vicinity of the airfield and guarded all the time. Storing them away from the airfields was also a safety measure in the event of German air raids.

During this time a special train was run for RAF personnel on Saturday and Sunday nights, leaving Lincoln at 10.30 pm and stopping at Five Mile House for RAF Fiskerton and at Bardney, Woodhall Junction and Coningsby for nearby airfields. Because there was only one crossover at Coningsby the engine would run to Tumby Woodside to run round its train, returning with the empty coaches to Lincoln. These services varied somewhat, sometimes also operating on Fridays and Mondays as well as the weekend, and finally on Saturdays only. Apart from offering the opportunity of a night out in Lincoln these trains would also serve personnel returning from leave.

Coningsby lost its goods facilities on 30th March, 1964. The station became unstaffed on 7th October, 1963 and total closure was on 5th October, 1970. These details apply to all stations along the 'New Line'.

The picturesquely named Tumby Woodside station looking west in August 1970, vegetation is already beginning to encroach across the platforms.   *P. Grey*

Tumby Woodside station, signal box and crossing looking east, still very much a GNR scene although the date is August 1970, just before closure.   *P. Grey*

Tumby Woodside

The station served a few houses scattered along an unclassified road. The signal box was built with the shallow pitched roof and tall operating floor windows typical of the later GNR style. The box stood at the eastern end of the up platform next to a level crossing, the gates of which were operated by a wheel in the signal box. Signalmen here included Jess Carrot, Bill Burrows and later Archie Blagg, who came to Tumby after being a telegraph lad at Spring Lane and remained until the end. The other man was Bill Vinters and Jack Scholey was the station master.

Opposite the signal box, on the down side, next to the crossing, stood the red brick booking office of the same pattern as others along the line. Such a building could never have been justified at such an isolated location. The entrance to the goods yard ran behind the office past a weighbridge office and the imposing station master's house, again both typical of the line. The goods siding was west of the platform on the down side. The station did considerable business in cattle, potatoes and sugar beet, local users included Messrs Sinclair & Co. of Mareham-le-Fen, millers and general farm merchants who received all their offals and cake from Grimsby and Hull.

The platforms at Tumby Woodside were brick faced with brick-built waiting shelters of a similar design to those at other stations on the line, the down shelter affording the luxury of a cast-iron fireplace.

New Bolingbroke

The village of New Bolingbroke was founded by John Parkinson, steward of Sir Joseph Banks. The new settlement, 7 miles south-south-west of Old Bolingbroke, was sited so that it could have water communication with Boston and the surrounding fens by means of navigable drains. There was a Bolingbroke fair, 'for pleasure and pedlery', held on 10th July. A Tuesday market was established in 1821 but soon became obsolete. By the mid-1850s the population was about 500 persons.

The station was situated at the southern end of the long straggling village, next to a level crossing. The general layout was similar to that at Tumby Woodside but the opposite way round, with the signal box on the down side and the booking hall on the up. A siding and goods yard was on the up side at the west end of the layout, an additional 385 yds-long siding was east of the crossing gates. The gates were worked by a wheel in the signal box. The box was manned by Bert Squires, Ralph Smith and L. Pettit.

There was a busy goods turnover at New Bolingbroke and many corn sacks were delivered to local farmers. The engineering firm of Rundles loaded scrap metal into wagons which were transported to Lincoln.

Harold Squires was born in New Bolingbroke in 1922 and lived in a row of cottages close to the station. Harold's father had helped to build the line and he lived long enough to see it removed. He maintained that the line had brought prosperity to many of the fenland villages north of Boston. Prior to the opening of the 'New Line' goods had to be collected from Dogdyke on the Lincoln-Boston line.

New Bolingbroke station looking west, the waiting rooms still complete with their canopies and everything looking very neat and tidy.   *D. Thompson*

The booking hall, signal box and crossing at New Bolingbroke, *c.* 1928. Some cattle are being driven down the road to the sidings east of the crossing. The booking hall survives as an antique shop called 'Junktion'.   *Wisbech & Fenland Museum*

New Bolingbroke signal box and crossing, the signal box is a good example of the later GNR box design. *P. Grey*

New Bolingbroke station looking west in August 1970, still looking well cared for, although the waiting rooms have lost their canopies. Note the down line laid with concrete sleepers. *P. Grey*

A GNR class 'A4' 4-2-2 No. 266, stands at Stickney station with a local train. No. 266 was the prototype of the class of 12 express engines built by Ivatt in 1898, the last batch of 4-2-2s built in Britain. The rest of the class were classified 'A5'. No. 266 was shedded at Lincoln in 1917 when the whole class was withdrawn which would indicate that this photograph is dated *c*. 1913 as both tracks are still in place.   *Author's Collection*

GNR class 'A4' No. 266, an Ivatt-designed 4-2-2, enters Stickney station with a train from Skegness just after the opening of the line.   *Author's Collection*

My early memories of the railway are of waiting for the 'Echo train', which brought the newspapers from Lincoln. These arrived at about 6.45 in the evening and were thrown out onto the platform in a bundle. I helped my elder cousin to deliver them in the village.

I remember the large number of excursion trains which used to thunder through the station at weekends on their way to Skegness from the Midlands. I used to lay in bed of a Sunday night and listen to them returning home, sometimes until almost midnight. There were also cheap excursions from the villages at weekends costing about one shilling return to Skegness.

The first station master I remember was Mr Lunn, who was there in the 1920s, then Mr Williamson, Mr Houlden, and finally Mr Oliver (who was the last station master on the line at closure). I recall the platelayers' trolley which they propelled along the line with a long pole, this was later replaced by a motorised version.

Coming home from school at lunchtime we had to hurry to get over the crossing before the gates closed. If the gates were closed we had to wait a few minutes for the midday train to pull out of the station. The engines seemed to be bursting with power as they moved off, hissing steam and coughing smoke, the crew usually waved to us.

In July scores of horses would arrive at the station from where they would be walked to Revesby Park ready for the Revesby Show. The arrival of the horses was a great occasion for us children, we sat on the grass and watched the proceedings.

My father used to send his Rhode Island Red poultry to various shows throughout the country via New Bolingbroke station. When they returned we used to search the hampers to see if they contained any prize cards. These were sometimes half-eaten by the prize winners.

My uncle, Arthur Squires, was a signalman and was accidentally killed by a train at Orgreave, near Sheffield in 1927. I think his was the only corpse to ever be delivered to New Bolingbroke station.

During World War II, I was called up to join the army and left New Bolingbroke station on 15th January, 1942, bound for Ipswich and eventually Burma. I arrived back on 14th November, 1946. Unfortunately I could only get a train from Lincoln as far as Coningsby that night so I had to walk, with my kit bag, from there to New Bolingbroke.

Stickney

The station served a large neat village, two miles east of New Bolingbroke, and was situated in a shallow cutting adjacent to the A16 roadbridge. The brick-faced platforms were sited to the east of the bridge. There was a slight variation in the station buildings here in that the booking hall was incorporated into the up platform waiting room, this had road access.

The signal box was west of the road bridge on the down side and controlled movements in the up side siding, which was alongside the running line and opposite the box. Signalmen were Teddy Long, Basil Danby and Eric Platts. Station master Fox was in charge during World War II, followed by G. Brown who was at Stickney for only a short while before being replaced by G. Blanchard, who was also the church organist.

The opening of the line was enthusiastically celebrated by the residents of all villages along the line, Stickney being no exception:

Great excitement prevailed in this village on Tuesday last, the occasion being the opening of the new line. The village was gay with flags, bunting, and flowers, almost every householder showing a brave display of colour. Amid the cheers of a large crowd and 130 schoolchildren, who had marched down to the station bearing flags and singing the National Anthem, the first passenger train steamed into the station at 9.07 am. Immediately following this train came a pilot engine which was gaily decorated with flags and flowers. Upwards of 100 tickets were issued during the day, a large majority going to Skegness, some of them in the first place having booked at Kirkstead and thence to Skegness, with the intention of travelling over the length of the new line. The fortunate possessor of the first ticket to be issued at this station is the popular rector, Rev G.H. Hales, who has daily watched the making of the line with the keenest interest. His intention is to have the ticket framed and no doubt it will be handed down to posterity as a memento of the occasion.

During World War II, Stickney village enjoyed the services of a church, a Methodist chapel, three shops, a garage, a pub, a school, post office, a doctor and a policeman. There was no electricity in the village, most houses using oil lamps and cooking on coal ranges or oil stoves. The station house and railway cottages all followed this pattern. The booking office was provided with a Tortoise stove, the porters' room had a coal range and open coal fires heated the waiting rooms. Other stations along the line, and the stations that served them, would be very similarly provided for at this time.

Next to Stickney station lived George Wright who had a smallholding and kept a cow, a pig and a few hens, as did many local people. The local butcher would slaughter the pig which would be hung in the kitchen to be used as required. During the War there were no street lights; local signposts and station nameboards were removed. Some farmers did not alter their clocks to correspond with British Standard Time but rather kept them the same all the year round.

Station master Fox was a Captain in the Stickney Home Guard. Sunday morning marches were carried out along the station approach road and exercises with Smith guns took place on Mr Herd's field. Ammunition was kept in Mr Silson's shed and a field near Hagnaby Lock was used for exploding grenades and sticky bombs. Exercises were also carried out with other units in the area, one such was based at Eastville station. On one occasion the station master there, Mr Smith, was demonstrating how a 68 grenade worked in the booking office. Unfortunately it exploded removing Mr Smith's arm and peppering the backside of the lad clerk, Albert Clements, with shrapnel.

The Stickney army cadets also met on Sunday mornings in the downside station waiting room.

During the 1940-45 period there were three passenger trains each way between Stickney and Lincoln running at 8.58 am, 1.11 pm, and 5.02 pm. Trains to Skegness ran at 10.09 am, 2.02 pm, and 6.40 pm, with slight variations from time to time. Two booked goods trains ran daily, 4247 down was due at Stickney at 7.00 am and 4261 up at 2.00 pm. The station was open from 7.00 am to 7.00 pm each day and was closed on Sundays and at all other times, with the exception of the movement of troop or other special trains.

The signal boxes at all stations along the line were open for the two goods workings. It was not unknown for goods trains to run very late especially as traffic for the aerodromes increased. Derek Fox recalled the latest down goods arriving at 2.00 pm and the up goods at about 5.00 pm. In order to avoid delay during air raids the boxes were required to be open as necessary to caution trains. Signal boxes were also required to open at night during periods of snow and ice in order to prevent the points and signals freezing up.

Stickney yard held 29 wagons. This was altered somewhat on a foggy afternoon when a long rake of wagons was being propelled back under the bridge into the siding. Unfortunately the engine driver failed to see station master Fox's hand signal or hear the three long blasts on his whistle due to fog and smoke under the bridge. When he did stop the siding capacity had been increased by four wagons. Firewood was plentiful for some time afterwards.

In order to release signalmen for station and yard duties Special Instructions authorised the signalman on arrival of the down or up goods, to give 'train out of section' to the box in the rear in accordance with Block Regulation 10, provided the train had arrived complete with a tail lamp. The box in the rear could then switch out of circuit. The signalman at the box receiving the goods train would 'Block Back' to the next box open, in accordance with Block Regulation 13, either 2 pause 4, if the train was inside the home signal or 3 pause 3 if the rear of the train was outside the home signal. When the train was standing at the down platform at Stickney or Coningsby it was outside the home signal. It was therefore strictly necessary, according to the Rule Book, to comply with Rule 178 clause C, which stated, 'should a train be detained at a station by station duties for a period 5 minutes beyond its booked time . . . at places were fixed signal protection cannot be afforded, the station master must arrange for the Guard, or some other competent person, to protect the train in accordance with Rule 179 . . . (etc.)' This rule was seldom complied with and would have been impractical at these two stations.

Goods traffic at Stickney consisted of potatoes, corn, hay, straw, sugar beet, seed potatoes, cattle, horses and coal for Bert Holdershaw, the coal merchant. Hay and straw was double sheeted and labelled, 'Lincoln to weigh'. A lot of the potatoes were loaded without destination to the order of Marshall Brothers of Bitterwick, Cooper Brothers, or Graves and Mobster of Boston, all of whom would perhaps delay giving a consignee for several days, by doing so using the railway as storage points. Most of the potatoes were consigned to Ruane, Kings Cross or Farringdon Street, London.

The majority of the outgoing traffic was delivered to the station by horse and cart. Small holders supplying sugar beet included Harry Silson, Bill Doncaster, George Heard and John Butler. When loading beet it was customary to place the wagons in the dock if possible to allow the them to throw the beet down into the wagons rather than having to throw upwards. This consideration often depended upon the relationship between the farmer and the station master! Most of the beet was dispatched to the sugar factory at Bardney. It was sent by permit which stated the dates upon which the factory would accept it. If the factory was short of work it would accept any permit date, this was known as 'free loading'.

On one occasion a person from Stickford consigned a donkey by train, it was to be loaded into a horsebox at Stickney station and attached to the rear of the 1.00 pm passenger train. However, the reluctant donkey was still approaching the station bridge when the one o'clock train was moving off beneath it. It was

Lincoln-based class 'B1' 4-6-0 No. 61405 at Stickney station with a train for Skegness on 6th July, 1952. *P.H. Wells*

Class 'K3' 2-6-0 No. 61938 arrives at Stickney station with the 12.03 pm service from Skegness to Sheffield Victoria on 11th July, 1959. *H.B. Priestley*

eventually persuaded to complete its journey to the station in time to be attached to the 5.00 pm passenger train.

During the War the staff at Stickney consisted of station master R.W.G. Fox, porter-signalmen Fred Long and Basil Danby and a carman, George Dixon. In April 1942 Albert Dixon, George's son, joined the staff as lad porter. Mr Fox's son Derek joined the team as lad porter on 3rd November, 1943, at the same time Albert Clements was transferred from Eastville (hopefully fully recovered from his painful accident described earlier) and took up the post of booking clerk. Basil Danby lived in the crossing house close by the up distant signal. Ted Long and George Dixon lived in the two cottages in the station yard. The station house was on a bank on the down side of the line adjacent to the bridge. In the yard there was a weighbridge with its office, a cattle dock and coalyard.

The whole of the Lincoln area at this time was under the control of E.J. Stephens, the district superintendent, who was located at Blankney and Metheringham; the district signalling inspector was Ted Harrison, who was stationed at Boston.

It was the practice of the guards on the first up passenger train and the down goods to changeover *en route*. Derek Fox remembered that some of the guards on the goods would drop a detonator into the brakevan stove timed to explode at the time his relief arrived in the van. Derek recalled a Skegness guard by the name of Bill Short, who sounds as though he would have been an unlikely victim of such a prank. Despite his name Bill was a massively built man who made a shunting pole appear as a matchstick in his huge grasp.

There were two manned level crossings between Stickney and New Bolingbroke and one towards Midville. Drinking water to manned crossings was supplied in metal containers and delivered by platelayers' motor trolley, or by the engine of a goods train. Signal boxes were also supplied in the same way. Special train notices and other messages were tied to a piece of wood and given to the guard of a passing train to throw out at the appropriate crossing as the train passed.

All of the crossings on the line were exempt from Rule 99 which stated, 'Unless special authority be given to the contrary, the gates at level crossings must be kept closed across the roadway, except when required to be opened to allow the line to be crossed'.

Derek Fox described a fire in the lamp room at Stickney station on 4th August, 1942:

My father had gone to Lincoln for the day, a relief station master, Cecil Cordell, from Lincoln, was in charge. At about 3.00 pm Albert Dixon rushed into the booking office to tell Mr Cordell the lamp room was on fire. Mr Cordell hurried to the pay phone in the booking hall and dialled the operator. She insisted that he paid sixpence for the call before she would put him through to the fire brigade. After a search for change Mr Cordell was eventually connected to the nearest fire brigade at Spilsby, eight miles away. By the time the brigade arrived the tarred, sleeper-built building was well alight. Adjacent to the burning building was a large oil storage tank. Ted Long opened the signal box to caution the 5.00 pm up passenger train and to instruct the driver to stop short of the building. The firemen used water from a deep well to the rear of the station to put out the blaze.

Lincoln-based class 'B1' 4-6-0 No. 61009 *Hartebeeste*, runs into Stickney station with a train for Skegness on 11th July, 1959; judging by the puddles on the platforms it is not the kind of day for visiting the seaside.   *H.B. Priestley*

A dmu leaves Stickney station and heads towards Midville just prior to the closure of the line. Grass is already growing on the down platform. The signal box can just be glimpsed through the bridge.   *M. Hall*

The function of the lamproom was the trimming and lighting of lamps, so the bench would have been well soaked with oil and very flammable. However the fire officer decided to put the cause of the fire down to 'enemy action'. No more was heard of the incident. A new brick building replaced the remains of the old structure.

Prior to the building of East Kirkby airfield, a mock airfield, complete with wooden planes, was sited at Hagnaby Lock. It was illuminated at night and was regularly bombed by enemy aircraft. RAF personnel would fill in the craters and make ready for the next raid. These sites were known a as 'K' sites.

On the night of 13th January, 1941, at about 9.00 pm, a bomb was dropped at Stickford, another on the road near Hagnaby Lock, a third bomb landed near the up Stickney distant signal in the middle of the track and not far from Basil Danby's crossing house, at which place it brought down the living room ceiling. John Ayres and his wife lived in a house situated between the signal box and the crossing, the blast knocked the back door out of Mr Ayres' hand and threw him across the road. The bomb crater was 50 ft across and 30 ft deep, the down line was cleanly cut and dropped into the crater; the up line too was cut and turned round towards the fence as if it had been laid that way. For the next week all down trains terminated and started from Stickney. Although, several wagon loads of ashes from Lincoln were dropped into the crater, the track sank by about two feet when the first train passed over the restored section. Ted Long, later declared: 'For them as don't believe pigs can jump, they should've seen mine when that bomb went off it jumped clean over its sty'.

The following year John Laing contracted to build a bomber airfield at East Kirkby. Most of the labour was Irish and Stickney station was used for the receipt of most of the building materials, the overflow being delivered to New Bolingbroke. Stickney siding capacity was only 29 wagons, Laing required 40 or 50 wagons of ballast a day in order to keep the cement gangs working. It was therefore suggested that additional sidings were constructed. A meeting on site between representatives of J. Laing, the district superintendent, the district engineer, the district inspector and station master Fox proposed constructing three additional sidings on the down side between the bridge to a connection with the main line behind the signal box. This would utilise the spare lever capacity within the signal box's 25 lever frame, numbers 4, 5, 6, 20, 21, 22. However, due to various problems, including the time it would have taken to construct the new facility and the fact that Laings could unload daily as many wagons as could be placed in the existing siding, it was decided not to proceed. The system was that a train of 40 wagons of ballast would arrive at the station, 20 of the wagons would be placed in the siding and would be emptied into waiting lorries in about 20 minutes. The empties were then shunted out and the remaining wagons moved into the siding. Sometimes the empties could be dispatched by the same train thus allowing ordinary goods and coal wagons to remain for unloading. Additional wagons were sent in special ballast trains, these being split between Stickney and New Bolingbroke. As well as ballast and sand from Bardon Mill, Scunthorpe and Navenby, iron pipes from Stanton, cement from Rugby and concrete pipes from Tallington were all shipped in through the station.

The aerodrome became operational on 27th August, 1943. From this time the

There is a desolate feel to this photograph of Midville station, with what is possibly a group of fishermen waiting for their train.   Here, as at Coningsby, the platforms are of wooden construction.   *D. Thompson*

A spartan looking Midville station, *c.* 1970.   The station waiting room canopies have been removed and the seat has lost its nameplate.   *Author's Collection*

railway brought in all materials and goods for the RAF. The down goods conveyed between 30 and 40 wagons of bombs from Swinderby daily. These would be spread between Coningsby, Tumby Woodside, New Bolingbroke and Stickney. Open wagons were used to transport high explosive bombs, box vans for fuses, incendiaries and ammunition. The big 4,000 lb. 'cookies' were loaded one per wagon. All wagons were code labelled and the movements sergeant would advise each station master which wagons were to be detached, sometimes exchanges of wagons would take place between stations. Bombs were unloaded by RAF cranes into their own transport

Goods for the airfield were collected from the station by the RAF transport section using long articulated vehicles. Apart from wagon loads of stores, tyres etc., the up goods conveyed up to five box vans, next to the engine, full of parcels and packages of every sort for delivery to stations along the line. At Stickney sorting the parcels and packages and unloading traffic for the airfield took up to two hours daily.

Quite a lot of goods traffic was passenger rated, on Tuesdays and Thursdays for instance, kippers and wet fish from Grimsby were unloaded from the first up passenger train. Scotch kippers were delivered off down trains. On Tuesdays and Fridays 50 or 60 boxes of Scribona cakes were received via the 2.00 pm train originating from Birmingham. If they missed the connection at Lincoln on Friday they would arrive on Saturday; this caused the early turn porter to miss the bus home to Boston. The train stood for 15 minutes while it was unloaded. Boxes and tea chests were taken off for the NAAFI 262676. All traffic received on down trains had to be barrowed across the line to the tranship shed. All this traffic was additional to the normal goods traffic loaded in the yard. The station carman George Dixon delivered to the RAF as well as delivering and collecting goods around the villages and farms in the area.

There were sad times when a van had to be provided for the conveyance of coffins. Derek Fox remembered an occasion when three coffins were loaded onto the 1.00 pm train. 'The RAF band played the funeral march and the bearer party slow marched onto the train, laying a Union Jack on each coffin. Sometimes coffins were pre-loaded and the passenger train would be set back into the siding to attach the van.'

Midville

The village is situated in the centre of East Fen, and the station was north of the village, alongside a minor road which followed the course of Hobhole Drain. The line crossed the drain, then the road on the level and ran into the station which was to the east of both of them. The familiar booking hall stood on the down side, next to the level crossing, with the signal box opposite on the up side. The red-brick station buildings were the same style as elsewhere along the line. The platforms here, as at Coningsby, were of wooden construction. There was a siding and small goods yard at the east end of the layout beyond the down platform. A further 369 yds-long refuge siding was provided to the west of the station beyond the road and the Drain. During 1941-1942 GNR Pullman cars were stored in the sidings at Midville in order to get them away

The bridge that carried the railway over Hobhole Drain and into Midville station. The booking hall is on the left and the down side waiting shelter is visible beyond the gates.   *P. Grey*

Midville station, signal box and crossing in August 1970, looking west; both roads are laid with concrete sleepers.   *P. Grey*

from Hornsey carriage sidings, in London. Station master Smith of Eastville was in charge and signalmen were Harold Wright and Roy Coupland. This was a busy station dealing with the usual farm produce, particularly potatoes and sugar beet. Fishermen from the Sheffield area came to Midville by train at weekends to fish Hobhole Drain.

Spilsby Road

Spilsby Road was a crossing over an unclassified road, a seven-lever cabin on the up side, just east of the crossing, controlling operations here. Mrs Gladys King was the signalwoman here.

Just after the introduction of the Derby lightweight diesel units into the area Arthur Motley was working an evening train from Lincoln to Skegness. The weather was appalling, with torrential, driving rain making the going difficult. The Spilsby Road distant signal, which was controlled by the crossing keeper, gave him a clear road but as he approached the gates Arthur saw them close and a bus cross the line. He jammed on the emergency brakes and got out of the driving cab as quickly as he could. The unit went through the gates. No one was injured but the top rail of one of the gates, complete with its lamp, were found laid across Arthur's seat. It later transpired that because the train was half-an-hour late the crossing keeper had assumed he had already gone through. When the bus appeared he did not consult his instruments and just opened the gates.

Bellwater Junction

Bellwater Junction came under the jurisdiction of Mr Smith of Eastville and was manned by Syd Mabbet, who later went to Eastville and was replaced by Sid Belk and Reg Stubbs, who was resident. Reg later moved to Sibsey and was replaced at Bellwater by Percy Laud. Sid Belk eventually moved to Willoughby, being replaced by Alan Bamber.

The box closed at 10.30 pm, the resident signalman taking care of the gates which led exclusively to farmer Stan Farrar's house and farm, which meant that the resident signalman was not troubled very often. When Bellwater was closed the block section was between Eastville and Little Steeping. Little Steeping box remained open from 4.00 am until 11.00 pm the 'block' then being between Old Leake and Firsby. Firsby South controlled the curve for Skegness trains but access at its west end was worked by the station box, which also controlled the line from Skegness into the station. Besides passing trains Firsby South box had to open to turn engines via the angle. The box was manned by H. Kinsley and later George Cargill and Ken Chester.

Firsby station box was a very busy place, signalmen included Fred Easter, Walter Rutter and Harold Roberts. The box closed after the departure of the Skegness engine for Boston and reopened at 4.00 am for the mail train. During World War II it was open continuously.

Firsby North was a 'no block' box which controlled a north crossover for the goods yard and main line and points for the bay (Skegness) platform to the main line to allow branch engines to run round their trains. These points were

Spilsby Road crossing cabin makes a nice little cameo in this May 1971 shot, the 'New Line' already closed.   *P. Grey*

A Skegness-bound dmu approaches the remote Bellwater Junction signal box on 19th September, 1981. The scene is little changed today, except that the fine GNR somersault down home signal was removed and replaced by an upper quadrant signal on 8th October, 1995.
C.A. Allenby

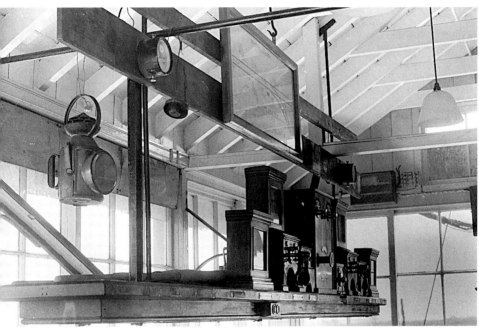

Bellwater Junction box instrument shelf and indicator board. *P. Grey*

Inside Bellwater Junction box showing the lever frame and writing desk. *P. Grey*

Bellwater Junction signal box looking north in August 1970; this was one of the most isolated situations on the GNR system.   *P. Grey*

The point where the 'New Line' joined the ELR at Bellwater Junction, seen here in August 1970. The isolated nature of the junction can be appreciated from this view.   *P. Grey*

Above: Inside Firsby station signal box on 4th August, 1964. A Skegness train has cleared the through road so Mr Moore resets the points, he is restoring No. 32, the main crossover. He has then to reverse 28, which does duty as a facing lock to both the through road (No. 29) and the Skegness bay to the up main crossover (No. 27), and therefore is normally reversed. The relief signalman is operating the gates. *G.H. Brown*

Right: The East home signal at Firsby with No. 5 pulled off for a local train to go to the station, Bank Holiday 1964. *G.H. Brown*

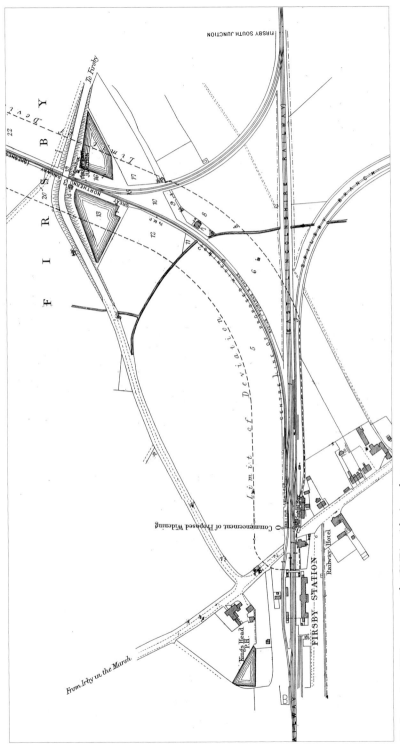

Firsby station, 1898 as seen on the GNR's widening plans.

A good view of the south end of Firsby station on 19th September, 1970, just before closure. The photograph gives a good sense of the rural nature of this busy station which even at this late stage still retains its essentially GNR character. The Skegness line is nearest the camera.
Author's Collection

A view of Firsby station looking north in May 1970; only the clothes worn by the waiting passengers confirm the date, the station remained essentially 'as built' throughout its life.
G. Goslin

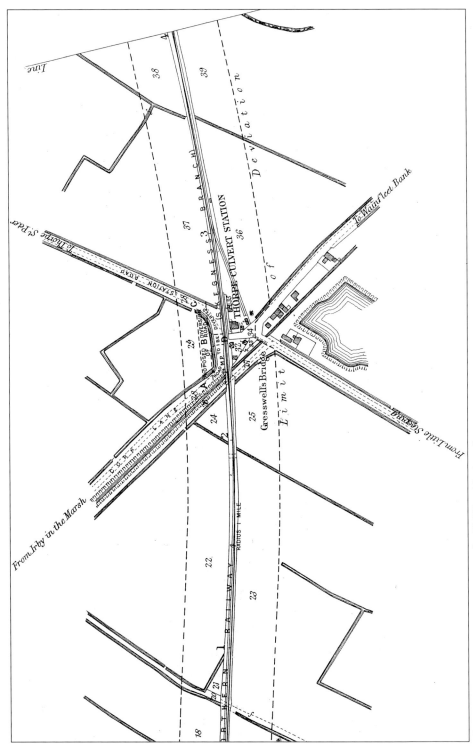

Thorpe Culvert station, 1898 as seen on the GNR's widening plans.

worked by porters with 'release' from the Station box as required.

Two groups of S&T men were based at Firsby, one gang under Jack Geary and Joe Blakey worked with an assistant between Firsby and Sibsey boxes and all boxes on the Skegness branch. The other gang of two men, George Clayton and Bill Dunk, worked the 'New Line' from Midville to Woodhall Junction.

The Skegness Branch

Thorpe Culvert

As a result of the 1900 doubling of the branch, a new down platform was built, 200 ft long and 12 ft wide, this included a general and ladies' waiting room and conveniences. At the same time an existing up side siding was lengthened by 165 yards and connected to the main line at the east end of the up platform; it was joined to both the up and the down lines, providing a crossover between the running lines by means of a slip point. The signal box at the west end of the layout on the up side had 19 working and 3 spare levers, as well as a gate wheel for operating the level crossing gates, which separated the box from the station. The box (normally only switched in for goods trains or to avoid delay) was worked by two porter-signalmen, one working 5.30 am to 1.30 pm and the other 1.30 pm to the finish. Harry Coe was at Thorpe Culvert for over 40 years and was resident at the house which stood over the road on the up side. George Rains began at Thorpe Culvert in 1942 and the station was under the authority of station master Lusher, at Wainfleet.

This was a busy station, dealing with potatoes, sugar beet and providing many sacks for farmers for the transportation of corn; the nearby estate of John Saul was a regular user of the railway facilities, so too the nearby Cranberry Farm and Bell Bros of Wainfleet Bank.

During the summer the signal box was often in use on Saturdays and Sundays for the passing of special trains to and from Skegness. Thorpe Culvert certainly kept its signalmen fit, the box being on the opposite side of the road to the rest of the facilities which involved a lot of to-ing and fro-ing.

An old gentleman who lived on his own near the station had a yearly season ticket valid between Thorpe Culvert and Skegness. He spent much of his time every day travelling between the two stations and was well known by the staff, drivers and guards, and was sometimes invited into the driver's cab. He would begin his travels on the 8.30 am from Thorpe Culvert, back on the 12.00 noon for his lunch; return to Skegness on the 1.00 pm and back again on the 4.30 pm. His last trip left Thorpe Culvert at 6.30 pm and he returned on the 8.30 pm; sometimes he varied the trains but not often. In the winter, or during bad weather, he would often remain on the train at Skegness.

The two level crossings between Thorpe Culvert and Wainfleet were operated by the wives of porters who lived in the crossing cottages. Thorpe Culvert lost its goods facilities on 27th April, 1964 and became an unstaffed halt on 7th October, 1968. In summer 1996 Timetable Thorpe Culvert was downgraded to the status of a request stop.

Thorpe Culvert station looking west, September 1964. The signalman's cottage stands at the end of the up platform with the signal box just beyond.   *D. Thompson*

The up side waiting shelter crossing and signal box at Thorpe Culvert on 17th March, 1995. The signalman's cottage has been demolished and rails lifted in the old goods yard behind the platform.   *Author*

Wainfleet

Wainfleet-All-Saints is a pleasant market town set in rich marshland and standing near the River Steeping, which starts its life as the River Lynn and finishes as Wainfleet Haven, where it joins the sea at Gibraltar Point, five miles east of the town. Originally Wainfleet was a Roman settlement called Vannona, at the sea end of the Salters Way, which linked the area with the Midlands. There were several potteries nearby and salt pans on the shore. A Danish barrow exists at Northolme and when the Wainfleet and Firsby Railway was in the process of construction, a great barrow in a field near the station was cut in two and found to contain seven singular graves, which were round in form but widened towards the bottom, they were lined with clay, which had been worked to a perfectly smooth surface. The space around contained cockle and mussel shells, fragments of bones and pottery; each grave appeared to have a double clay floor, the uppermost being concave and three inches in thickness.

William Waynflete, who gave Oxford Magdalen College, gave Wainfleet the Magdalen College School, in 1484. Standing near the river, this remarkable two-storeyed building has two eight-sided towers flanking the west front, one contains a superb newel staircase, the other an ancient bell.

Wainfleet was the original terminus of the railway until the opening of the Skegness extension in 1873. In 1883 , because of increasing holiday traffic, an up extension line was added at Wainfleet, at the same time the station was resignalled. The layout was controlled by two signal boxes, East, at the station, and West which stood beside a level crossing west of the station and was used to cross trains during the busy summer season. At this time the layout at Wainfleet included an up siding and goods shed and an engine shed which was behind the platform at the west end.

The sharp curve to the east of the level crossing was responsible for an accident in the summer of 1880:

An accident occurred on the GNR on Thursday evening between Firsby and Skegness, which resulted in serious injuries being sustained by several passengers who were journeying from Skegness to Nottingham. The train was the Thursday afternoon special, which runs from Nottingham to Skegness and back, and, as usual, there was a large number of visitors to the seaside who took tickets by it. The train had 8 or 10 coaches and left Skegness on the return journey at 8.00 pm. All went well until Wainfleet was approached, when, at the spot where there is a sharp curve, the first coach left the rails followed by the remainder of coaches. As soon as possible passengers made their exit from the coaches, all of which maintained an upright position.

It was then found that in several cases the shock of the event had produced serious injuries. In one coach Mrs Oram, wife of Mr W. Oram, Poultry dealer of Bottle Lane, Nottingham (who also has a shop in Skegness), was travelling with some friends and her condition was such as to create alarm. Mrs Coxon of Sneiton, who was also a passenger in the same compartment was also injured.

In 1891 the Board of Trade served the Firsby & Wainfleet Company with a Notice to provide block working and interlocking. This was curious as the company had adopted these from the opening of the line and its inspection in

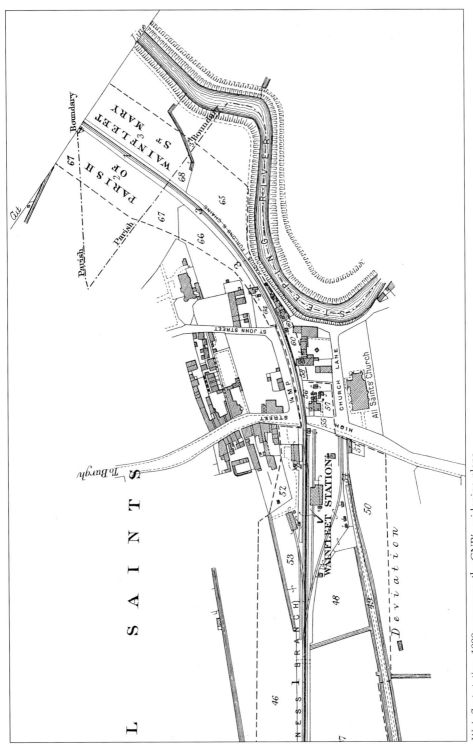

Wainfleet station, 1898 as seen on the GNR's widening plans.

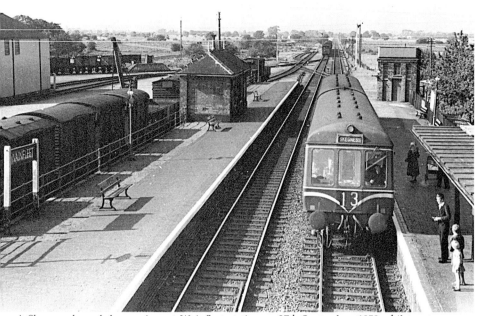

A Skegness-bound dmu arrives at Wainfleet station on 27th September, 1958 whilst a steam-hauled goods train heads off in the opposite direction. This photograph taken from the footbridge gives a good idea of the facilities available at Wainfleet. *H.B. Priestley*

An unidentified Standard class '4' 2-6-0 shunts the goods yard at Wainfleet on 27th September, 1958. The goods shed can be seen behind the train and the station, complete with footbridge, in the distance. *H.B. Priestley*

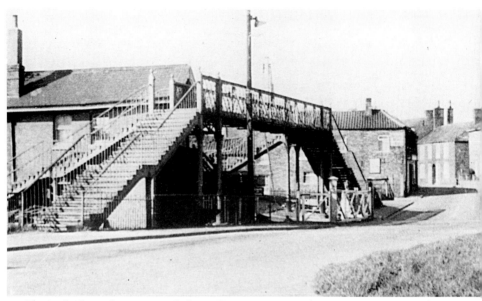

The footbridge at the eastern end of Wainfleet station, notice the two sets of stairs on either side of the line, one from the platform, the other from the street.   *Wainfleet Museum*

A photograph taken to mark the closing of the coal yard at Wainfleet, *left to right*, Messrs Richardson, Metcalf, Allenby, Blades.   *Wainfleet Museum*

1873. On 20th October, 1891 the company Secretary, Mr Patterson, wrote to the Board of Trade saying that the company Chairman, James Martin, had died on 24th August and that a previous letter by the deceased had been written 'under a misapprehension'. He went on to say that as the block system and interlocking had long been in place, no expenditure was entitled under the Order, and that, 'the Directors do not propose to carry out any of the works referred to'. This letter was 'noted' by Major Marinden on 22nd October and marked 'put away'.

The Board of Trade's full resignalling proposal had included moving the lines at the west further apart, a new loop and platform at the station, with a new signal box built on the platform, also a new goods shed coal stages and sidings. When one considers these proposals it is no surprise that the Wainfleet company rejected them and opted for a 'simple resignalling' scheme.

Also contained in the original Board of Trade proposals were plans to abolish the existing 1873 signal boxes at the rest of the stations which stood at the end of platforms, near to level crossings (with the exception of Thorpe Culvert which was across the crossing opposite the station). These boxes were each to be replaced with a new structure on the opposite side of the crossing as at Thorpe Culvert. However, when the line was doubled in 1900 there was no mention of new boxes being brought into use at the other stations and the boxes remained in their 1891 positions, albeit with larger frames. At the time of the doubling the East box at Wainfleet was referred to as the 'existing box', even though it had only just been built. This was because it had been brought into use controlling the old layout whilst the old box was being demolished. West box appears to have been a ground level cabin, similar to that at Bellwater on the East Lincolnshire line, with a lever frame alongside the cabin. It would seem that the box disappeared with the doubling of the line, although this is not specified in the proposals.

When the line was doubled a new up platform was built, and the original brick-built goods shed demolished to make way for it. The new goods yard layout included a new shed constructed of corrugated steel. A footbridge was also included in the 1900 alterations, standing next to the level crossing and signal box; this was removed in 1969. The station house and offices remained pretty much the same from the opening of the line. The waiting room and booking office were contained in a single-storey extension at the eastern end of the station master's house, a canopy running the length of the house and the extension. On the up platform a single-storey brick-built waiting shelter was provided of similar design to others along the line.

Agricultural traffic consisted of potatoes, sugar beet and wagon loads of celery in the season. The yard was provided with a cattle dock, coal siding and a 3 ton 12 cwt crane. The railway lorry was driven by Joe Houlden.

G.W. Lusher succeeded Mr White as station master in 1947 and was there into the 1960s, Ray Griggs was the chief booking clerk at Wainfleet for many years; Doreen Rook was passenger clerk and Doreen Teesdale worked in the ticket office in the mornings and the goods office in the afternoons. She remembers Mr Lusher's method of paying wages was to have a tobacco tin for each person into which their wages were put, the tin handed to the employee, emptied and

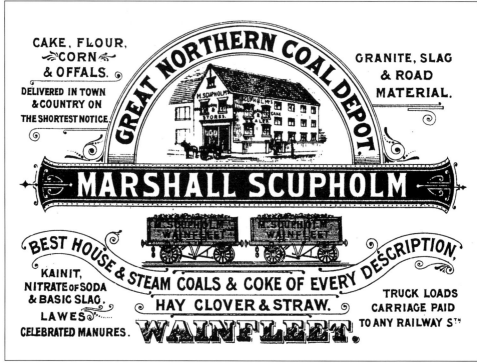

Scupholm's publicity dating from 1902.

A delivery lorry belonging to Scupholm's, coal merchants in Wainfleet. *Scupholm's Collection*

returned for the procedure to be repeated the following week. Chief goods clerk was Stan Chamberlain, who succeeded Mr Plowright in the 1960s. Mr Chamberlain liked to work 'by the book', which proved difficult after Mr Plowright had run the department in his own idiosyncratic way for many years previously.

The signal box was worked in two shifts from 5.30 am until 1.30 pm and from then until 'finish', usually about 11.00 pm. Signalmen were Bob Baxter, Norman Pratchett, Percy Lord, and Ted Green. The box worked in circuit with Firsby and Skegness, except at weekends and required weekdays, when Thorpe Culvert and Havenhouse boxes were in use.

Porters were Messrs Rollinson, Buttery and Smith. One of two platelaying gangs was based at Wainfleet. These men under the supervision of Bill Carrot and his deputy Mr Green, worked to Thorpe Culvert and the Skegness side of Havenhouse. The other gang was based at Skegness and worked from there to where the Wainfleet men finished.

Chain Bridge level crossing was about half-a-mile beyond the sharp curve out of Wainfleet station and was, for a good number of years, operated by Ken Rook. The crossing was protected by distant and stop signals, the signals being worked by the crossing keeper from a four-lever ground frame installed in 1898.

Wainfleet closed to goods traffic on 2nd May, 1966, the event reported in the local press:

The 94 year association between Scupholm & Son, coal merchants of Wainfleet, and the railway came to an end on Friday when the last coal wagon was shunted into the Wainfleet siding, and the last scheduled goods train to travel the Firsby to Skegness line moved on its way to Skegness.

Skegness and Wainfleet are two of the goods depots that were closed by British Railways on Saturday, 30th April. The others in the area were Alford, Burgh-le-Marsh and Willoughby. In future all goods which these five depots received will all have to go by Louth or Boston.

Scupholm's have been the main users of the Wainfleet depot since the railway from Firsby to Wainfleet was completed in October 1871. The firm was founded in 1845, but until the railway was built coal was brought to Gibraltar Point by their own schooners and transported up the river to Wainfleet in barges. They were the first tenants of the goods yard soon after the railway was completed and, on Friday, became the last. In the time that they have been transporting coal to Wainfleet the railway has carried nearly a million tons of coal for Scupholm's and, up to last week they were bringing in about 80 tons a week by rail.

As he was watching the last wagons shunted into the siding, Richard Scupholm, who is the head of the firm now, reflected with his oldest employee, Walter Richardson, who has been with the firm 44 years, about the quality of coal today in comparison with the past. Waving a hand towards the wagons he said, 'Coal like that would just have been sent straight back years ago, but you just can't get the sort of coal they had then'.

Mr Scupholm will now have to arrange other means of transporting his coal. Some will be transported all the way from the collieries by road, and some will be transported to Lincoln by rail and then brought to Wainfleet by road.

Wainfleet station became an unstaffed halt on 7th October, 1968. In the summer of 1996 Wainfleet saw a reduction of three trains a day on Monday to Fridays.

An aerial view of Wainfleet taken on 31st June, 1976.   The railway curves through the photograph from the top right-hand corner. Wainfleet station and goods yard can be seen just before the line curves sharply towards the bottom of the picture.   *University of Cambridge*

Wainfleet station in September 1964. The steps of the footbridge can be seen on the right. Note the front valancing of the platform canopy has been removed. *D. Thompson*

Wainfleet engine shed and water tower seen here in the 1930s. The shed has a set of doors in the back wall which are not apparent in the pre-1900 photograph. The severity of the curve just beyond the level crossing at the far end of the station can be judged by the position of the building, apparently occupying the trackbed, just beyond the crossing gates. *Lens of Sutton*

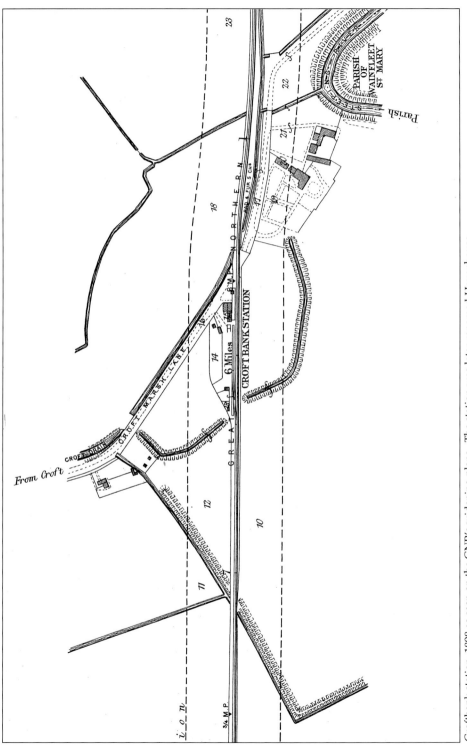

Croftbank station, 1898 as seen on the GNR's widening plans. The station was later renamed Havenhouse.

Wainfleet Engine Shed

The engine shed at Wainfleet was built by the Wainfleet & Firsby Railway and was operational by September 1871. The brick-built, single road structure measured 54 ft x 20½ ft. It had a single-pitched, slate-tiled, gable roof. A double door arched entrance was at the western end of the shed, the rear wall was provided with a square framed small-paned window. The side walls were subdivided into five 10 ft bays, sections two and four including arch-topped small-paned windows.

Coal was supplied from a small platform next to the shed entrance. Water was drawn from a well and stored in a 2,500 gallon water tank which sat atop a 11 ft 8 in. square brick-built tower which stood on the platform next to the shed entrance. The tower was divided into three bays on each side, with a door in the east end and windows placed at the top of each bay, above eye level. The water tower carried the station nameboard, just below the windows on the south side of the building.

Because of the cramped situation of the engine shed a short siding was installed to facilitate the coaling of engines in November/December 1911, at a cost of £15. The original request for such a facility had been made by the local engineer on 2nd March, 1903 and approved by the Way & Works Committee, at an estimated cost of £80.

Subsidence affected the rear wall of the engine shed, so much so that, in 1912, two timber buttresses were put in place to shore up the wall. Soon afterwards an arched doorway, identical to the existing one, was created making the shed a 'through' type with a short track extension beyond the new rear door. It seems that re-roofing took place at the same time. This may have been linked to a fire which took place at the shed at a date which has yet to be established. The legend has it that the fire brigade arrived and ran out their hoses along the platform only to find that they were the wrong way round and had to be reversed before they could begin to deal with the fire.

The two engines stationed at Wainfleet were changed every three days, replacements coming from Boston. The frequency of these changes was necessitated by the poor quality of water at Wainfleet which caused rapid scale formation and priming thus precipitating frequent washouts. It was estimated that during the period 1901-1906, 325,000 gallons of water a year was provided at Wainfleet Shed. When the shed was demolished is not clear but evidence points to 1956-57 at which time the water tower became the signing-on point.

Havenhouse

Originally known as 'Croftbank', the station was enlarged and renamed on 1st October, 1900 and included a new up platform with a brick-built, slated, hipped-roof waiting shelter. At the same time the down platform was extended. A signal box stood next to a road crossing at the east of the layout, on the down side. The road was unclassified, and, beyond the crossing, became a private road leading to Jack Measures' farm. Although the road led to Gibraltar Point and its bird sanctuary, Jack Measures used his authority to close

An unidentified class 'K3' 2-6-0 approaches Havenhouse station from Skegness in September 1964 watched by a group of fishermen on the down platform. *D. Thompson*

An unidentified class '31' approaches Havenhouse station, with a train from Skegness on 10th July, 1965. The private road leading to Gibraltar Point Bird Sanctuary can be seen beyond the crossing gate. Although the station is still open every railway item in this delightful scene has disappeared, with the exception of the platforms. *J.S. Gilkes*

Havenhouse up platform waiting room flanked by GNR cast-iron railings. *Author*

A general view of the interior of Havenhouse signal box on 13th October, 1985.

Adrian Vaughan Collection

Tiny Seacroft station in September 1964. Although the buildings are in similar style to the others along the line the platforms are very short.   *D. Thompson*

Class 'K3' 2-6-0 No. 61816, a Colwick engine, approaches Seacroft station from Skegness on 6th September, 1952. The small loading dock serves the siding running alongside the down line.
P.H. Wells

the private road gates to the public on summer Bank Holidays, which no doubt pleased the signalman who had no need to operate the crossing gates. Many thousands of corn sacks, from the Lincoln sack depot, were delivered in van loads for Measures Estates. They were collected from the station by men using horse or tractor and carts. Other farming companies in the area were C.W. Parker and Worth Farms. The latter ran a 2 ft gauge light railway over three miles of track running between fields and crossing the River Steeping by a 60 ft-span steel bridge, then following the river to Havenhouse station. Here a siding brought the light railway up to the level of the standard gauge wagon bottoms. The line was laid with rails 5½ yards in length, laid at 3 ft spaces on 4 ft-long pressure creosoted sleepers. Metal spreaders were bolted to the bottoms of the rails, these had a slight adjustment. Each section was joined by fishplates and the whole secured to the sleepers with dog spikes; a Dorman Simplex petrol driven engine was driven by Albert Miller and was capable of pulling 15 tons in dry conditions. It was eventually sold to Messrs Granthams, builders, in Skegness, for use in their brick pits. The light railway transported potatoes, corn, hay and straw bales to the station returning with 200 tons per annum of seed potatoes and artificial manure from Kings Lynn. The little railway opened in 1927 and closed in 1968-69.

Havenhouse had two porter-signalmen who worked 5.30 am to 1.30 pm and 1.30 to close. Syd Booth spent 36 years working on the branch, all but 10 at Havenhouse. At one time he and his father worked in shifts at the station; his wife's grandfather helped to build the line. Leading porter-signalman P. Dawson worked on the branch for 19 years.

An accident happened near Havenhouse station in 1912, as an excursion train made its way from Horncastle to Skegness. Six-year-old Jessie Caborn was sitting on a passenger's knee when her attention was drawn to some cows in a field. She jumped down and ran to the carriage door. No sooner did she touch the door than it flew open and she vanished.

The engine driver happened to be looking in that direction and saw the child fall. He pulled up as soon as possible, and, as the train slowed, 30 or 40 people jumped onto the line. Had a train been passing in the opposite direction there would have been a catastrophe. The passengers found Jessie dazed and bruised but otherwise none the worse for her experience. The young lady was examined by a doctor on arrival at Skegness; he pronounced her well enough to go for a paddle in the sea.

Havenhouse closed to goods traffic on 15th June 1964 and became unstaffed on 7th October, 1968.

Seacroft

Opened as 'Cowbank', taking its name from a small drain that runs alongside the road leading to the station from Wainfleet Road, the station was renamed 'Seacroft' on 1st October, 1900. Here were two short platforms, which, like others along the branch, were surfaced with blue bricks. The station house stood at right-angles to the line on the down side and alongside the signal box. A typical brick-built and slated single-storey waiting room occupied the up side

A variety of horse-drawn vehicles stand outside Skegness station waiting to meet passengers off incoming trains.   *Winston Kime Collection*

A busy station concourse at Skegness in 1911.   *Winston Kime Collection*

platform. The platforms were lit by paraffin lamps, the lamps in the station house and waiting rooms were oil-lit. The station was never served by mains electricity or water, water being brought in from Skegness by rail.

The last station master was W.J. Smith, who held the post in the 1930s, with Mr Smith's departure Seacroft came under the jurisdiction of Wainfleet.

The signal box was often switched in on Saturdays and Sundays during the summer. The box closed after 'out of section' had been received for the No. 5 (7.45 am) down goods until 12.00 noon, and again after 'out of section' for No. 15 (12.50 pm) up passenger train to about 8.05 am the following day. It also opened as required to prevent the delay of trains.

This was a bleak, isolated place, the village of Seacroft being no less than 2½ miles from the station and better served by Skegness so passenger traffic was never very significant, although it did improve somewhat when the LNER installed camping coaches in the siding for the accommodation of holidaymakers. In 1938, 150 people used Seacroft, the figure having fallen to seven in the two months prior to closure to passengers on 7th December, 1953.

The last two men to work at Seacroft were Ted Green and Aubrey Cram. The two porter-signalmen worked a two shift system from 5.45 am to 10.45 pm. Only five trains a day stopped at the station at this time, two up and three down. Ted Green and his wife occupied the station house, Aubrey travelled daily from Skegness.

Mr Searby, of nearby Marsh Farm, used the station to transport his pedigree Lincoln Red bulls. Mr J.K. Measures transported potatoes and corn through the station, much of his incoming seed was delivered there too.

Goods traffic ceased on 27th April, 1964. The signal box lost its frame and became a crossing keeper's refuge; the gates were operated manually, Seacroft continued to be a manned crossing until 1980 when the wooden gates were replaced by an automatically controlled crossing.

The station buildings, which had become a pets' crematorium, burnt down after a day's business in 1978. The remains, along with the down side waiting room were demolished, the up side facilities having being removed some time previously.

Skegness

The original station at Skegness had four platforms, six carriage sidings and a turntable. Beyond the buffer stops was an open concourse and station offices. The cost of construction was in the region of £9,000.

On the first Saturday of its opening the GNR ran a cheap day excursion on the new line to Skegness. The train ran from Lincoln, dropping many people at stations along the way to spend the day with friends and family. About 300 passengers arrived at Skegness. Complaints were made at the level of fares published by the GNR, the dissatisfaction stemming from the premise that they were too high, and that it was cheaper, and just as quick to travel by rail to Burgh-le-Marsh and from there take a conveyance to Skegness.

A mishap occurred at Skegness station later that year:

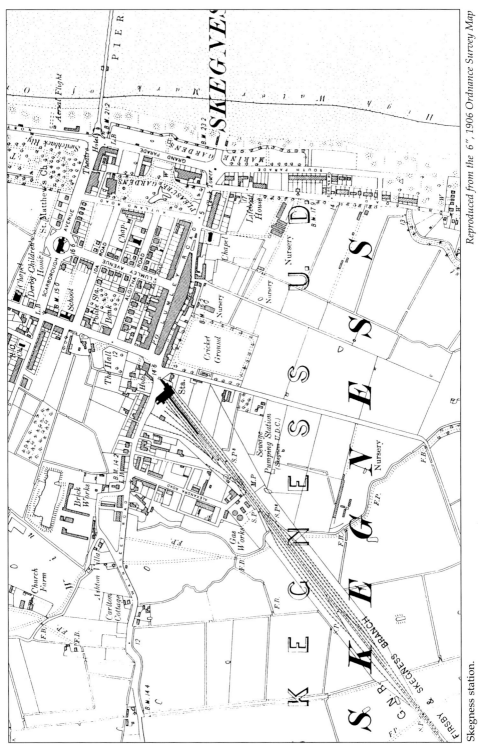

Reproduced from the 6″, 1906 Ordnance Survey Map

Skegness station.

As an excursion from Gainsborough and Lincoln was leaving the platform a few minutes after 7 o'clock the engine, on reaching the first points, ran off the rails, its wheels instantly embedded in the sand, which brought the train to a sudden stand. The engine of the Boston train in the rear was detached and went to the aid of the disabled engine, endeavouring to pull back the tender which was still on the rails. This was done on the supposition that the engine would thereby regain the metals. After several tugs the stricken engine was in a worse plight than before, the worst of it was that it blocked the two trains behind it. Both trains were full of passengers and the delay had seen all Boston excursionists return to their train, which was timed to leave at 8.00 pm. An ordinary train was standing in another platform, awaiting the departure of the two excursions. When the time arrived for this train to set off, to meet the mail at Firsby, it was speedily taken possession of by the afrighted excursionists, a large number of whom thus reached Firsby, where, shortly after the despatch of the mail, they were sent forward to Boston. The rest of the excursionists reached the same point some time later. It is worth noting that although the line is a single one between Firsby and Skegness there is no telegraph as yet, and it appears there was no means, on Saturday evening, of sending for help from any distant quarter, a defect that will no doubt be remedied with as little delay as possible.

Unfortunately not so.

The limitations of the provision at Skegness was soon felt. A newspaper report in the summer of 1874 stated,

Skegness was crowded on Monday beyond all precedent. The area over which people were spread is so large that it was difficult to form even an approximate estimate of the number present. It may assist readers to form some idea when we state that no less than 10,000 were conveyed. To this number must be added the thousands that went on foot or in vehicles. The sports took place in a field at the rear of the Vine Hotel. Access to the race ground could only be obtained by crossing a huge sewer. Instead of a decent bridge, a few old boards were laid across the bottom and people had to step down the bank on one side and scramble up the other as best they could. The arrangements of the GNR for receiving and despatching the trains were as complete as they could be with the limited accommodation inseparable from a single line of rails. The company have provided immense sidings at the station and the wisdom of such a course was manifest on Monday evening, the dispensing of the crowds in four or five directions in search of carriage accommodation effectually obviating any serious crushing. Up to 8.50 pm the trains were got off on time but after that time the 'Excited' portion of the excursionists had to be dealt with and they were not so easy. The last batch got off between 10.00 and 11.00 pm. No accidents. Telegraph communication with Firsby would have greatly facilitated their arrangements and enabled the to do their work more easily.

Later the same year a further report confirmed that still nothing had been done, 'Skegness still has problems. They need telegraphic communications. At present to telegraph to any part of the country must either travel or send a message to Wainfleet or Burgh'.

In 1898 Lord Scarborough agreed to provide land for the enlarging of the station, which was in conjunction with the doubling of the line (completed in 1900). The new layout included a new island platform and improved refreshment rooms. A roof was erected over the passenger concourse. The concourse stopped short of the station master's house, which stood at the

The station master and two of his staff sit on the concourse at Skegness station in the early 1900s.
Winston Kime Collection

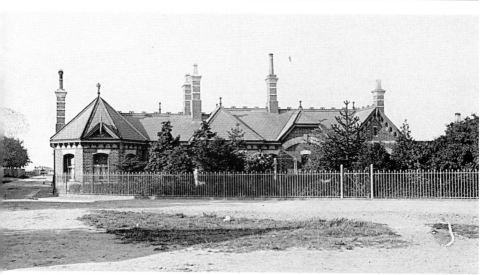

A 1921 view of the station house at Skegness, the home of station master Chambers. G.W. Chambers had been station master at Ludborough, Heckington, Bardney and Littleworth before moving to Skegness.

Frank Gelder

Skegness station staff on 18th March, 1921, with station master G.W. Chambers in charge.

Frank Gelder

Skegness station, note the addition of the triangle.

Reproduced from the 6", 1946 Ordnance Survey Map

junction of Richmond Drive and Wainfleet Road. A later extension of the concourse boxed the house uncomfortably into the corner of the junction.

The final layout at Skegness provided seven platforms and 12 carriage sidings on either side of the running line, a total of 24. The 12 known as the 'Northern Group' were numbered one to twelve from the running line outwards; the same applied to the 'Southern Group' except that number one was also known as Cowbank Road this became an extended spur and was effectively South No. 13, running in a westerly direction alongside the running lines. There was also a shorter southern and a northern spur at the western end of the layout. The sidings were separated from the station and its immediate environs by a four line 'throat'. The connections between the Northern and Southern group of sidings were worked by a 10-lever ground frame, situated at the west end of the sidings alongside the down main line.

An engine line ran at the rear of platform seven and beyond it a further line served the coal yard. A turning triangle was installed in about 1949, to turn engines too large for the turntable. This followed a £10,000 expansion scheme in the mid-1930s to enable Skegness to cope with the new holiday traffic bound for Butlin's Holiday Camp which opened in 1936. A water crane and a coal and ash stage were provided along the base of the triangle. The turntable was north of the running line along an engine road which left the throat and crossed the gas works siding, which ran off to the west. Here too were provided coal and ash facilities. Five goods sidings were numbered starting from the outermost and fanned out north of platform one. Number five ran to the cattle dock and was served by a yard crane. Number four ran to the goods shed.

The signal box was situated beyond platform three, at the Wainfleet end; it was worked in two shifts, 5.30 am to 1.30 pm and 1.30 pm to 'finish', which was usually about 11.00 pm after the arrival, at 10.30 pm, of the last train from Firsby and the departure of its engine to Wainfleet (later Boston) depot. Originally the box was classified 1 in the summer and 2 in the winter. Strangely, when traffic declined and the status of a box was decided by equipment rather than by train movements, Skegness was designated 'Special A'. Under Railtrack it is grade 4. Signalmen here have included Alf Knowles, Albert Naylor, Alan Burkitt and John Cussons.

Station staff in living memory have included station master Jim Howden, who was the kind of man that if you had nothing to do you looked as though you had. He was at Skegness for many years and was followed by George Edenbrow, who was the last station master at the resort. In the 1950s and 1960s there would be about 50 people working at the station between May and September, half of them employed only for the summer season. Station foremen were Jim Reeson and Jack Wright, porters included Jack Merrick, Harry Webster and Bob Young; passenger clerks were Walt Craven, Reg Harcourt, Ron Mountain, Kay Mitchell and Tom Gelsthorpe, who could tell passengers how to reach anywhere in the country without referring to a timetable. Goods clerks were Jock Grant, Mrs Cave and, in the winter, Ron Mountain, who moved from the passenger side to goods. The goods yard was the domain of head shunter 'Pop' Waumsley, Percy Reeson, Charlie Smith and Arthur Cobb.

LNER class 'B8' 4-6-0 No. 5280 awaits departure from Skegness station with the 7.50 pm to
Bulwell Common on 3rd June, 1934.   *LCGB/Ken Nunn Collection*

Class 'J6' 0-6-0 No. 3629 on the turntable at Skegness on 10th June, 1935.   *Ray Stephenson*

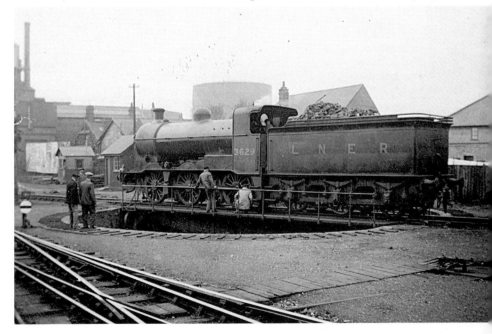

Class 'B4' 4-6-0 No. 6104 stands buffer to buffer with Class 'D2' 4-4-0 No. 4324 at Skegness on 7th August, 1939
C.S. Bayes

An unidentified 'Black Five' stands in platform 5 with an excursion train in September 1964; modern traction is in evidence in the next platform.
Real Photographs

A busy scene at Skegness in 1952. Three 'B1s' await departure along with Colwick-based class '39' No. 64827.   *Peter Holmes*

A good view of Skegness station in the early 1950s with the crew of Colwick-based class 'K3' 2-6-0 No. 61826 relaxing after the journey to the seaside. The coal is moved forward on class 'B1' 4-6-0 No. 61056 whilst an unidentified member of the same class prepares to move out of the station and into the sidings.   *N.E. Stead*

Platforms one and two at Skegness station occupied by a delivery of caravans. Also in view are the goods shed and yard crane. *Peter Wombwell Collection*

A Land Rover is used in a rather crude fashion to unload caravans at Skegness. *Peter Wombwell Collection*

The concourse at Skegness station with a good display of hanging baskets.   *Author's Collection*

Skegness station concourse in September 1964 with W.H. Smith's bookstall in evidence and a sign announcing 'Buses for Butlins Camp'.   *D. Thompson*

Goods traffic coming into Skegness included coal, tranship goods, containers for Butlin's Camp. A considerable amount of corn was sent out. Fish was delivered from Grimsby on the back of the 2.20, 5.20 and 9.50 pm services and from Hull at 6.35 pm. Wednesdays saw the delivery of boxes of cakes from Lyons in London, on Thursdays, Scribona cakes came from Birmingham and on Fridays Lyons and Walls ice cream. Friday also brought tons of luggage sent on by holidaymakers in advance of their arrival the following day.

Lorry drivers included Harry Ainsworth, Sid Costel and Fred Blades on the goods side and George Smith, George Merroney, and, in the winter, Tom Needham moved from the ticket office to the delivery of parcels. Delivery routes encompassed the Lumley Road, Drummond Road area; Roman Bank, North Parade and Burgh Road; Winthorpe, Ingomells and Chapel St Leonards, and a daily delivery to Butlin's Camp in the summer. W.H. Smith's bookstall at the station was run by Mr Martin. He was followed by Willie Stoneham who had worked there since a boy.

On 27th April, 1966 the engine road and turntable were taken out. The following year, on 12th March, the goods yard and platform one were removed from service. Shortly after, the Southern carriage sidings and associated signalling were removed, presumably the turning triangle also disappeared at this time. Towards the end of 1985 the large curve into platform six was lifted and the line taken straight into the main line.

The splendid buffet on the station was closed in October 1983, the sorry saga being reported in the local press:

The Travellers Fare buffet at Skegness railway station will close next Saturday despite attempts to keep it open.

Manageress Mrs Jan Robinson, whose family has run the buffet for more than 30 years, has applied to take over the lease but all she has heard is silence from the British Railways Property Board.

This week she has been busy trying for a reprieve on the closure and asked for a temporary lease to be issued. Travellers Fare say the buffet is a loss maker, so what makes Mrs Robinson want to take it over? 'I believe that we can make the buffet pay as a family business. We wouldn't have the massive overheads that a company like Travellers Fare has to suffer', she said.

Mrs Robinson accepted that times would be hard for the buffet during the winter but in the summer season profits from the increased number of rail travellers and trippers would more than compensate. 'My Mother (Mrs Webster) ran the buffet for 25 years before me. It has become a family way of life. At times my husband and other relatives have helped out. Skegness station needs a buffet, it hasn't even got a proper waiting room. People come in here, not only for something to eat and drink, but for a warm and a chat'.

The closure came under fire from the South East Lincolnshire Travellers Association. The Association's Secretary, Mr Peter Wombwell, said that it would be the loss of a very useful facility. 'What is particularly annoying is the way the closure has been kept very quiet by Travellers Fare, even though the buffet was under review at this time last year. Presumably this was done so not to arouse any public objection. I hope that the buffet building will not become another derelict part of the station. At the time of writing this history that is indeed what it has become.

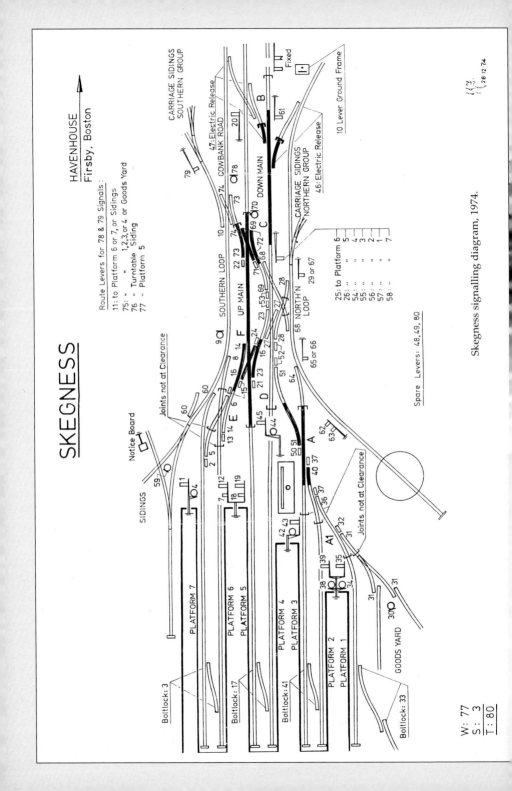

Skegness signalling diagram, 1974.

Skegness signal box and platform ends looking towards Firsby, seen here on 10th June, 1984.
Adrian Vaughan

The ticket barrier at Skegness station; notice the blackboard price list for the pay train service, 1*s*. 9*d*. to Wainfleet and 5*s*. to Boston. *Author's Collection*

Present staff at Skegness are John Thornley, Ian Cunningham, Dave Tuplin, Terry Hooley and Janine Miles; signalmen are Alan Burkitt and John Cussons. Skegness station continues to be a good transport interchange, the adjoining bus station providing regular services to Funcoast World (Butlin's), Ingoldmells, Chapel St Leonards, Sutton-on-Sea and Mablethorpe.

The 'Jolly Fisherman' is seen on the station concourse in May 1995.   *Author*

Chapter Nine

Rail Closures in Lincolnshire

Some North Lincolnshire branch lines had suffered closure prior to the Beeching proposals of 1963. Spilsby had lost its passenger service in 1939 and had closed completely on 1st December, 1958. The Horncastle line closed to passengers in 1954 but continued as a goods only line until April 1971. The Louth-Mablethorpe section of the old Mablethorpe Loop closed completely on 3rd December, 1960.

The first casualty of the Beeching proposals was the Woodhall Junction to Boston section of the Lincoln to Boston line, which closed to passengers and goods on 17th June, 1963. British Railways also suggested the closure of the Lincoln to Skegness line to take effect from 6th June, 1964. This would have seen the closure of the 'New Line' as well as the remainder of the Lincoln to Boston line. There was a strong feeling that this was the thin end of the wedge and that the Grimsby to Boston line was also under threat and with it the lines to Mablethorpe and Skegness.

The biggest local enquiry held by the Transport Users' Consultative Committee (TUCC) took place in Skegness on 15th and 16th September, 1964 to hear objections to the proposals and in particular the threat to the Grimsby, Boston and Peterborough main line. Two MPs for the area, Sir Cyril Osborne and Sir John Maitland were among the first to voice their opposition. Sir Cyril said that he had recently travelled through Lincoln by car and had been held up for some time at a level crossing, '. . . if this proposal is carried out and more trains are diverted through Lincoln then God help the people of that city so far as traffic is concerned'. Sir John Maitland expressed his opposition saying the loss of trains would cause unemployment and loss of trade both at the seaside resorts and in industry.

The case for Skegness was based upon a report prepared by Mr Milton Turner, Clerk of the UDC and put to the meeting by Mr Edwin Jowitt:

If British Railways have their way people living outside the cities will change into crofters who will flock to the cities and leave their rural areas to stagnate. In an age when travel is likely to increase at a great rate it seems odd that one of the largest counties in the land will lose the greater part of its rail system. The effect of these proposals will be to leave the greater part of Lincolnshire with no rail service. It will not merely be an amputation but a disembowelment of the rail services in this large county.

Mr Jowitt maintained that the proposals would mean that Skegness would now be 23 miles from the nearest station. He also accused British Railways of deliberately running down the services on lines it wished to close in order to strengthen their case for closure. He estimated the closure of the railway to Skegness would cost the town in the region of £1,250,000 per annum in lost revenue. This was based on a survey which showed that 57 per cent of the families who travelled to Skegness by rail would not came again if the line was

A Lincoln-bound train approaches New Bolingbroke station from Skegness on 16th
August, 1968. *J.S. Gilkes*

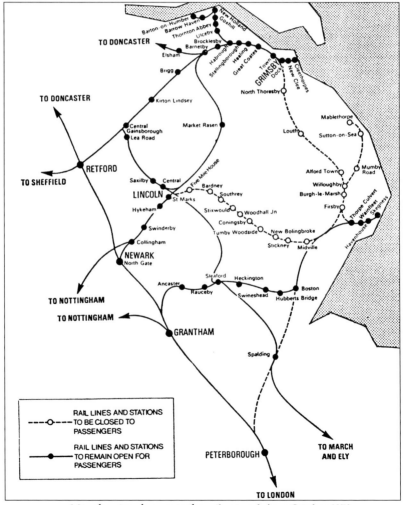

Map showing changes to the rail network from October 1970.

closed. The closure would also mean 25 per cent less for traders in the town, which could, in some cases, turn profit into loss. He continued, 'It is desperately important to get a larger conurbation in East Lincolnshire but first you have to attract industry and commerce'.

The point was also made that if the railway closed anyone wishing to be in London by 11.00 am would have to travel from Skegness overnight and pay an extra £4. Problems on the already congested roads would be made much worse by the influx of more road users. Shoppers going to Grimsby or Lincoln would find an increase in journey time with speeds being reduced to as low as 8 mph.

Mr G.R.S. Pepler, the Deputy Clerk of Lindsey County Council, said the County Council would not be objecting so strongly if the road programme planned over the next 15 years was in place before the proposed rail closures. As it was, further traffic on roads, already at their designated capacity, would impose further strain and hardship on those using the roads.

An interesting point was raised by the Deputy Town Clerk of Grimsby, Mr N.J.L. Pearce, 'A close relative travelled last week from Kings Cross to Grimsby and was charged 12s. 6d. more than the usual fare. When he enquired why this was so, he was told that the Grimsby train now travelled via Lincoln, hence the fare increase. My relative argued firmly and was able, in the end, to persuade the ticket clerk that the nearest way to Grimsby was via Boston. If the ticket clerk was acting in accordance with instructions then I think it is a most unfortunate way of proving a case'.

Mr Pearce also pointed out that the journey times by bus from Grimsby to Mablethorpe would be increased by 20 to 25 minutes over the time by rail, and to Skegness by more than an hour.

Mr Roy Maltby representing Butlin's Holiday Camp suggested that 50 per cent of the holidaymakers would refuse to travel by road resulting in a loss of between £250,000 and £300,000 to Butlin's.

Mr F.M. Wright, the Doncaster divisional manager, replied on behalf of the British Railways Board (BRB). He maintained there were two distinct problems, rural transport and holiday travel. As far as local journeys were concerned he felt the Board had tried to meet the requirements of the regular traveller in the proposals. He agreed that many would suffer 'some inconvenience', but said that the number who found it impossible to get to work would be comparatively few. He denied there had been an attempt to run down the services to strengthen the Board's case. The number of people travelling by rail to Skegness had declined since 1957, the main reason being that more people had their own cars. He felt it was wrong to expect the Board to go on providing rolling stock, permanent way and signalling to meet just a peak demand for weekend summer movement. He was confident that the diminishing demand would be adequately met by bus and coach operators.

The finding of the meeting were submitted to the Transport Minister who concluded that the BRB should re-examine its proposals. This it did and in due course once again proposed closure, this time with the exception of the Skegness line. A second TUCC inquiry was held at Skegness in May 1968, lasting for two days. The findings were again submitted to the Transport Minister who this time supported the Board's proposals. He felt that costs in

Firsby station on the last day of operation, 3rd October, 1970, with the 4.29 pm to Peterborough on the left and the 4.24 arrival from Skegness on the right.   *Lawson Little*

The last through train from Skegness to Grimsby departs at 10.50 am on 3rd October, 1970, formed by Nos. E50047/E56010.   *Lawson Little*

the region of £700,000 to retain the existing rail provision in Lincolnshire could not be justified because of the low usage and the considerable route mileage involved. He observed

. . . that most of the people using the Lincoln-Firsby services either travel the whole length of the line from Skegness or use the stations at Bardney, Woodhall Junction or Coningsby to travel mainly to Lincoln. Very few people use the other stations on the line and he agrees with the Committee that because of this their retention cannot be justified. The Minister accepts the Committee's view that having regard for the bus services at present available, augmented as proposed by the Board, passengers travelling on the Coningsby-Lincoln section would suffer inconvenience amounting almost to hardship if this section were closed and that those having to change buses at Horsington would suffer additional hardship. But he also noted that the numbers concerned were small and, bearing in mind the generally quicker though more expensive alternative rail service which would be available for travellers via Sleaford and Boston the Minister does not consider that he would be justified in asking the Board to keep this particular service in order to avoid the difficulty at Horsington.

The last day of operation over the condemned Lincolnshire lines was Saturday 3rd October, 1970. The lines closed included Lincoln-Bellwater Junction (via the 'Lincolnshire Loop' and the 'New Line'), Peterborough-Spalding-Boston, Firsby-Grimsby, Willoughby-Mablethorpe. Lawson Little visited the area that day and made notes. I think it is worth presenting in its entirety if only to emphasise the scale of the loss to Lincolnshire. Remember too, that in order to complete what he did he had to miss out the section from Peterborough to Boston.

I worked out an itinerary comprising: Lincoln straight through to Skegness; Skegness to Grimsby; Grimsby to Willoughby with a trip down the Mablethorpe branch; back to Firsby and finally return to Lincoln. This was one of several circuits and it was amusing to note that during the course of the day I seemed to meet other enthusiasts going the other way every time I changed trains.
My first journey was on the 8.34 am from Lincoln to Skegness, a through working originating at Sheffield. This arrived promptly in the shape of a six car dmu towing a parcels van. But despite the large number of passengers waiting, authority decreed that two cars would be sufficient, and by the time we had all been herded into the front two cars and the train split, we were 17 minutes late. The train consisting of Derby-built twin Nos. E50047 and E56010 was driven quite energetically along the riverside line due east from Lincoln, but the frequent stops and speed restrictions made it difficult to regain lost time.
It was a cool, clear autumn morning, and already the fishermen were busy along the river. At each stop we dropped off one or two more, each one wondering no doubt how the replacement bus service would cope with rods and baskets the following week. At Bardney there was activity of a different kind, this was sugar beet harvest time and the factory alongside the station was working flat out with clouds of steam rising into the sky and a small green diesel busy in the crowded sidings moving rakes of vans. On again to Southrey, Stixwould, Woodhall Junction, with the still extant Horncastle branch swinging in from the north. More quiet country stations on the southern edge of the Wolds, Coningsby, Tumby Woodside, New Bolingbroke, Stickney, Midville, the fact that our path was now protected by a continuous string of GNR somersault signals only seemed to emphasise how time had stood still in this quiet corner of Lincolnshire.

The last train from Firsby (dept 5.03 pm) to use Bellwater Junction, here running onto the 'New Line' bound for Lincoln: vehicle Nos. E56027/50027/50134/56205. The date, 3rd October, 1970.
Lawson Little

Approaching Coningsby station from the east, the signal box now badly vandalised, in October 1970.   *B. Wilkinson*

The sequence of rural names was nicely rounded off at Bellwater Junction, where we joined the main line for a short distance to Firsby, the junction for the Skegness branch. The direct south to east connection was out of use on this day, although fated to become the only survivor of the triangular junction within a few brief hours. We pulled into Firsby station before reversing down the branch. With the arrears reduced to 10 minutes we set off again towards the sea, its approach marked by shingle ballast and seagulls following a lineside plough. Soon that well remembered landmark, the Skegness gasholder, appeared ahead and we were passing empty carriage sidings and entering an equally deserted station.

Although the gasholder still stood much else had gone, the turning triangle for steam locomotives, the goods yard and most of the station canopies. It was the end of the season and only a crippled coach occupied one deserted platform. We were still 10 minutes late on arrival and only had time for a quick look around the station before buying a ticket for Grimsby. By this date there was only one through train each day from Skegness to Grimsby, and this left at 10.50 am, so even at this early stage I was 'closing the door' on a Lincolnshire rail service. We left punctually in the same twin unit dmu in which I had arrived, one noticeable benefit of these reversible trains was the facility for planning intensive useage on a complex route pattern; I was to renew my acquaintance with the same train again during the course of the day.

Retracing our steps to Firsby, we struck off northwards on the splendidly aligned and maintained main line which enabled us to travel at a steady 60 mph between stops, Burgh-le-Marsh, Willoughby, Louth where once 'C12s' simmered outside the shed, and soon, three minutes early into Grimsby.

My way lay south again, through Louth to Willoughby and promptly at 1.20 pm we drew out, yet again with the same dmu I had ridden from Lincoln five hours earlier. This time we had a CCT hitched behind us. Our speed was distinctly leisurely back to Louth and two minutes were dropped to Willoughby, no time to look round this delightful country junction as a cross platform connection was made with a waiting branch train for Mablethorpe. We were bustled into another Derby twin, Nos. E50011 and E56011, which left immediately on the short journey to Mablethorpe.

This fast connection was typical of working organised in the last years of operation, and it was often possible to see three trains simultaneously at Willoughby and elsewhere. It seemed strange to reflect that despite the bustle here, within a few hours not only would the branch close but also the main line south of Louth.

The branch line to Mablethorpe seemed to give a distinctly rougher ride than elsewhere, suggesting that maintenance might have been run down in anticipation of closure. However we safely reached Sutton-on Sea with the curiously named 'Tramway Crossing' a solitary memento of the long-gone Sutton and Alford Tramway, and soon into Mablethorpe, once a through station with the line continuing northwards and eventually returning to the main line just south of Louth station. Mablethorpe like Skegness, gave a distinct impression of 'end of season' and since the train didn't return for over an hour I had ample time to take a walk along the deserted beach.

The casual atmosphere of the branch seemed to have affected punctuality also and our planned departure at 3.52 pm was delayed, for no obvious reason, for five minutes before we set off on our bumpy journey to the mainline. At Mumby Road, a small halt, we stopped, there was no one on the platform, either passengers or staff, the guard looked out, rang the bell and we moved on. Thus ended, unobserved and unsung, 80 years of service.

At Willoughby our connecting train for Firsby was another Derby twin, this time Nos. E50019 and 56001. What a fascinating place Firsby was. In 1970 the Victorian overall roof still stood over the platforms which had once bustled with passengers from four directions, platforms alongside which had seen GCR 'Pom Poms' hurrying with packed trains up and down the Skegness branch, 'C12s' chuffing hoarsely about on locals, where 'K2s' and 'K3s' hurtled south with endless fish trains for the Capital.

In anticipation of the crowds, for this was the very last train along the 'New Line' towards Lincoln, the train had been strengthened to four coaches, a Met-Camm. power car No. E50134 joining Derby units Nos. E50027, E56027 and E56205. And hereby arose a snag. Because the two twins were not corridor connected, the rules decreed that two guards should be carried and as the time for departure passed we learned that the extra man was coming up on a Grimsby-bound train due at 5.08 pm. Unfortunately for timekeeping, this train, formed of our old friends No. E50047 and partner, limped in at 5.20 pm, obviously the earlier effort with the CCT had had its effect, as it was working on one engine only, departure was not made until 5.30 pm.

Soon we were slowing for the sharp curve at Bellwater Junction, the last train to do so, we were rewarded with a wave from the signalman and a string of detonators. On we went through the gathering gloom. At Bardney we met the last eastbound train to Skegness, a crowded twin unit carrying many local people out for a final trip, many of these transferred to our train to return to the city whose Cathedral now stood golden against the sunset ahead. On now past the deserted river and, all too soon, we were running into Lincoln Central station, some 10 hours after our morning departure.

The other passengers soon drifted away and after a while the train, which was working through to Sheffield, pulled out, no longer a 'last train' but just another cross-country dmu. The station was almost deserted and I walked out to the car as the last day in Lincolnshire came to a quiet close.

The derelict Coningsby Junction signal box on 27th October, 1970. The 'New Line' goes off to the left, the GNR Loop line to Boston went off to the right following the course of the River Witham. *R.B. Wilkinson*

Chapter Ten

The Present Day

The present day Skegness branch continues to make its own history. Leaving Boston station a single track heads north, crossing the River Witham by the Grand Sluice bridge and curving north-east onto what used to be the second longest stretch of straight line in Great Britain, on the old ELR between Boston and Burgh-le-Marsh. The line passes over Maude Foster Drain and several level crossings in quick succession and crosses Cowbridge Drain. At Sibsey trains slow to 15 mph for a junction where the line becomes double track. Sibsey station was closed to passengers on 11th September, 1961, although there is now local interest in reopening it.

The train picks up speed and crosses Hobhole Drain and passes the remains of Old Leake station, closed to passengers on 17th September, 1956. Crossing Spilsby Road the line passes through Eastville station, closed in 1961. Next is Bellwater Junction signal box, where nothing can be seen of the former 'New Line' trackbed which has all been returned to farmland in the vicinity of its former junction with the ELR. After Little Steeping station, which closed in 1961, the train crosses the River Steeping and slows to 15 mph in order to negotiate the south curve at Firsby, which leads to the Skegness branch proper. The trackbed to Firsby station and the Spilsby branch have virtually disappeared, the remains of Firsby station a pathetic remnant of its former self.

The branch heads south-east over Lymn Bank level crossing and arrives at Thorpe Culvert station, which, being close to the River Steeping, is still popular with fishermen. The station buildings are still intact and in good repair.

Beyond Thorpe Culvert the line crosses Wainfleet Haven 'New Cut', crosses Brewster Lane and Matt Pitts level crossings and makes its way across Wainfleet Connon before arriving in Wainfleet station. The site of the former goods yard is now a housing development.

Leaving Wainfleet the line curves sharply to the left (a 15 mph restriction) and heads north-west, passing Chain Bridge level crossing and crossing Wainfleet Haven 'New Cut' for a second time shortly before arriving at Havenhouse station, served only by a very basic one up and two down trains daily (in 1997). The station has lost its somersault signals and signal box and crossing gates but presents a tidy appearance and, like other stations along the branch, still retains its GNR cast iron railings. Gentle reverse curves take the line through Crofts Marsh, passing the site of Seacroft station, which closed to passengers on 7th December, 1953.

Skegness comes into view, a large amount of unoccupied land on either side of the line indicating the site of the former carriage sidings. Of the original 24 sidings only three of the Northern group remain, these were used for running-round and stabling locomotive-hauled trains, now a thing of the past at Skegness.

In 1977 British Rail introduced an economy measure in order to save on the wages of signalmen and crossing keepers. The idea was to open the Boston-

Thorpe Culvert signal box and station looking east on 10th June, 1984 with somersault signals still intact. *Adrian Vaughan Collection*

A view of platforms and signalling at Skegness with a good complement of visiting engines on 10th June, 1984. *Adrian Vaughan*

A snow plough at Skegness on 16th January, 1987 powered by two class '31s'. On 12th January the 5.56 pm arrival had been stranded at Skegness and remained there until the line was cleared. It then operated the 9.05 am to Boston on the 19th. *Peter Wombwell*

A train from Crewe is seen arriving at Skegness on 1st May, 1995. *Author's Collection*

Havenhouse station on 17th March, 1995; the crossing gates and signal box have gone and the elegant somersault signals are replaced by colour lights.   *Author*

Wainfleet station building and down platform, the different coloured brickwork indicating the position of the missing canopy. The miserable 'bus shelter' looks very out of place in this 1995 view.   *Author*

Skegness section for only 10 hours each day, employing just one man per box or crossing. Early morning and late evening trains were replaced by limited stop buses, connecting with trains at Boston. As usually happens these buses were not popular with passengers and were eventually withdrawn. The implementation of the 10 hour day was not without its teething problems. On the first Spring Bank Holiday after the establishment of the new system, the last train had to leave Skegness station at 7.20 pm in order to allow the signal boxes to close at 8.00 pm. Unfortunately four evening specials had been timed to arrive at Skegness after the 7.20 deadline. The signalmen were eventually prevailed upon to stay and deal with these trains but were far from happy about it. From May 1989 the section reverted to two shift operation, restoring early morning and late evening trains. This was made possible by a seven year agreement, jointly financed by British Rail and Lincolnshire County Council, to automate most of the level-crossings on the branch.

Other signs of modernisation include the equipping of permanent way speed restrictions with large new number signs, incorporating advance warning boards linked into an audible warning system. Large aerials have been erected at Boston and adjacent to the signal box at Skegness, to enable train drivers to be in radio contact with the signalmen at boxes which remain in use.

During the last 20 years various classes of locomotives have visited Skegness. A Boston-based class '03' visited the resort on at least two occasions, on one of these a steam crane was hauled. Class '20s' provided the motive power on excursions and scheduled services, these were usually double-headed but failures resulted in the occasional lone working, other combinations included treble and even quadruple-headed trains. Class '20s' have been seen latterly on weed-killing trains. Class '25s' were fairly frequent visitors on scheduled services, always double-headed. Class '31s' were regular visitors to the resort on scheduled services and occasional engineering trains, and sometimes double-headed. The only appearance of a class '33' was on a 'Jolly Push-Pull Fisherman' on 8th January, 1994, which featured Nos. 33 109, and D6535, 'Hertfordshire Rail Tours', with a 4TC set. Class '37s' were, at one time, seen frequently on scheduled services, often the Sundays-only from Cambridge, also on occasional excursions.

Class '40s' were regulars on the Saturdays-only Manchester services. Class '45s' appeared frequently with scheduled services and excursions. On 5th June, 1982, No. 45 020 piloted No. 31 190 when trains were running about one hour late. No. 45 006, *Honourable Artillery Company* was observed on 12th June, No. 45 055, *Royal Corps of Transport* on 14th June, No. 45 064 on the 17th and 18th June, No. 45 126 on 20th June and No. 45 125 on 27th June of that year.

From 4th to 12th July, 1982, no locomotive-hauled trains ran to or from Skegness, a limited service of dmus to Grantham being provided. Proper services were restored on 19th July. No. 45 075 was seen on 27th July and No. 47 083 *Orion* on 7th August. On 28th August, No. 40 061 appeared and No. 47 193 worked in the next day No. 47 144 appearing on 11th September. Indeed class '47s' were regular visitors on excursions, scheduled service and engineering trains, class '46s' less so.

The first ever visit of a class '55' ('Deltic') was on an excursion on 13th

The first ever arrival of an HST at Skegness with an excursion train from St Pancras on 22nd February, 1992 with No. 43051 in charge. *Raymond Wombwell*

Wainfleet signal box on Friday 17th March, 1995. The box is little changed but the goods yard is now a housing development. *Author*

August, 1978. After this they could occasionally be seen on the Kings Cross Saturdays-only trains.

The one and only visit of a class '56' was when one of the type worked as a replacement locomotive on a 'Jolly Fisherman' excursion. Other once-only visitors included a class '58' and a HST, both on railtours.

The much heralded replacement of conventional dmus by class '150', '153' and '156' 'Sprinters', with the introduction of new timetables on 11th May, 1992, was a let down because Boston did not receive its full complement of one '156' and three '153s' until the following day. The class '153' on the 6.37 am from Boston on the first day became so full when it approached Nottingham that the collector found it impossible to issue tickets. A similar single '153' on the 10.43 am from Skegness was 'full and standing' and was replaced on the next day by a conventional dmu.

The class '153s' proved scarcely more reliable than the dmus they replaced, cancellations, resulting in bus substitutions, were frequent, as many as three times a week. Their introduction was not without humour. The couplings of the 'Sprinter' family and those of conventional dmus are not compatible. On Saturdays the 8.00 pm and the 8.41 pm arrivals at Skegness, both dmus, were diagrammed to couple up to form the 8.49 pm departure to Nottingham. On 23rd May and again on the 13th June, one was a 'Sprinter' and the other a 4-car conventional dmu, with the result that one had to return to Nottingham as empty coaching stock, much to the chagrin of its driver, who had expected to ride home 'on the cushions.'

The summer services in 1992 saw a mixture of stock used including 'Sprinters' and 3- and 4-car dmus, as well as the old 2-car units. The 10.24 am (10.55 SO) from Skegness was usually composed of a pair of class '153s' which returned as the 4.10 pm (SO) arrival. This split at Skegness to form the 4.37 pm (SO) to Doncaster and the 5.19 pm (SO) service to Nottingham.

Some trains at Skegness did not make an immediate turn-round so there was often the pleasurable sight of four trains standing in the platforms.

The 9.49 am (SO) through 6-car dmu from Scarborough to Skegness was not proving to be as popular as the former through locomotive-hauled train from Newcastle, nor was the 10.01 am (SO) Skegness to Doncaster, which replaced the 10.21 am to Newcastle, although the Newcastle passengers, by changing at Doncaster, saved an hour compared to travel on the previous through services. Many Newcastle and Scottish passengers were being routed via Grantham in each direction.

The last down weekday train from Nottingham to Skegness, which formerly came through from Birmingham New Street, did keep better time in its revised form. Although the Working Timetable showed this train originating and terminating at Crewe this was not the case, the 3.48 pm (SX) from Skegness terminated at Nottingham. Arrivals and departures at Skegness during the summer of 1992 showed 17 arrivals and departures Monday to Friday, 26 arrivals and departures on Saturday and 9 arrivals and departures on Sunday. On May and Spring Bank Holidays, the locomotive-hauled excursion from Derby was hauled by a pair of class '20s', on both occasions the locomotives were Nos. 20 090 and 20 132. On Spring Bank Holiday, the excursion from

A class '150' 'Sprinter' stands at Platform 4 on 1st May, 1995. *Author's Collection*

The first train departing from Skegness to Mansfield for over 30 years. Class '150' No. 150 002 also provided the first train from Mansfield on the same day. It is joined to a Crewe-Skegness unit at Nottingham for the Nottingham-Skegness portion of the route, part of the 'Robin Hood' line services. *Peter Wombwell*

Sheffield was hauled by a red class '47', No. 47 489, with six Mark I and II coaches. Steam returned to Skegness in the form of preserved British Railways class '4MT' 2-6-4T No. 80080, on 10th April, 1993. The train departed Nottingham at 9.25 am and worked to Skegness via Sleaford and Boston, arriving at the seaside at 11.55 am. A Skegness to Boston return shuttle was operated leaving Skegness at 12.50 pm and returning at 3.10 pm. The return journey to Nottingham began at 3.55 pm and arrived at 6.15 pm. A further excursion with No. 80080 took place in 1993, followed by a trip behind No. 80079 on Easter Saturday, 1994. All excursions were met by the 'Jolly Fisherman' and the Skegness Silver Band.

In 1995 the Skegness-Crewe service operated hourly, with connections at Sleaford for Peterborough and London and also for Lincoln. Some trains called at Grantham. As soon as the hourly Crewe service was announced the South East Lincolnshire Travellers Association (SELTA) pointed out to the head of Tourism for East Lincolnshire District Council that Derby has a population of 215,000, Stoke-on-Trent 250,00 and Crewe 48,000 and that Stoke has connections every few minutes with Wolverhampton and its population of 255,000, and further, that both Crewe and Stoke have connections with the whole North West of England, with a population in the region of 10 million people. Moreover, the connections with Birmingham are increased by an hourly service to Derby. Lastly the traditional holiday destination for the Potteries has always been North Wales, with through train services, now however, the only resort with a daily through train service from the Potteries was Skegness. It is hoped that heavy advertising in the Potteries, with offers of concessions and discounts, will induce increasing numbers of people from the area to visit Skegness. It is suggested that the route may be named 'The Jolly Fisherman Line'.

During the early part of 1996 the Skegness branch became the victim of heavy snow, resulting in the suspension of all services during one Saturday. The following day locomotive No. 37 164 with snowploughs attached travelled to Skegness to clear the route, after which normal service resumed. This was the first time for many years that a locomotive of this type had been seen in the resort. The year 1996 also saw the introduction of a new through train service on Saturdays, the 7.00 am from Great Malvern to Skegness, calling at Worcester, Birmingham New Street, Burton-upon-Trent, Derby, Nottingham and thence via the Grantham avoiding line to Sleaford and Boston, arriving in Skegness at 11.25 am.

The prospect of privatisation will no doubt bring new challenges to those who fight to keep the line to Skegness open: good luck to them.

Signal Box Opening Hours, etc.
1897 and 1912

These extracts are from the GNR Appendix to the Book of Rules and Regulations and to the Working Time Tables, the first dated 1st November, 1897, the second 1st June, 1912. There are some interesting place name changes (*) as well as an additional signal box at Wainfleet west crossing, later Mat Pits Lane crossing. It would appear that this box disappeared when the line was doubled in 1900.

Skegness Branch

Distance from Firsby Jn	Stations, siding & signal boxes	Closed
	(1st November, 1897)	
1 46 ¼	Limb Bank road crossing	
2 21	Thorpe Culvert box	Open only under special notice
2 21 ½	Thorpe Culvert crossing	
2 22 ¾	Thorpe Culvert station	
3 62 ½	Wainfleet Road crossing	
3 62	Wainfleet West crossing	
3 62 ½	Wainfleet West crossing box	Open only under special notice
4 15 ½	Wainfleet station	
4 18 ½	Wainfleet box	Nightly 8.00 pm to 5.55 am; 8.00 pm Saturdays to 5.55 am Mondays. Open for early and late specials
4 18 ½	Wainfleet crossing	
4 47	Masons lane crossing	
5 79	Croftbank station	
5 79 ¾	Croftbank box	Open only under special notice
6 1	Croftbank crossing	
8 1 ¼	Cowbank crossing	
8 2 ¼	Cowbank box	Open only under special notice
8 2 ½	Cowbank station	
9 4 ¾	Skegness box	Nightly after last train is out of section to 6.10 am; after last train is out of section Saturday to 6.10 am Monday. Open for early and late specials.
9 17 ¼	Skegness station	
	(1st June, 1912)	
1 46	Lymn Bank road crossing	
2 21	Thorpe Culvert box	Week nights after last train is out of section to 5.50 am, after last train is out of section Saturday to 5.50 am Monday
2 21 ½	Thorpe Culvert crossing No. 17	
2 22 ¾	Thorpe Culvert station	
3 6 ½	Brewster Lane crossing No. 19*	
3 61 ¾	Mat Pits Lane crossing No. 24*	
4 15 ¼	Wainfleet station	

Distance from Firsby Jn	Stations, siding & signal boxes	Closed
4 17 ¾	Wainfleet box	Week nights after the last train is out of section to 5.55 am; after last train is out of section Saturday to 5.55 am Monday. To be opened for early and late specials
4 18 ½	Wainfleet crossing No. 26	
4 47	Chain Bridge Lane crossing No. 27*	
5 78 ½	Havenhouse station*	
5 79 ¾	Havenhouse box*	Week nights after last train is out of section to 8.00 am; after last train is out of section Saturday to 8.00 am Monday
6 1 ¼	Havenhouse crossing No. 32*	
8 1 ½	Seacroft crossing No. 39*	
8 2	Seacroft box*	Closed during winter months.
8 3 ¼	Seacroft station*	
9 4 ¾	Skegness box	Week nights after last up passenger train is out of section to 6.05 am; after last passenger train is out of section Saturday to 6.05 am Monday. To be open for early and last specials.
9 17 ½	Skegness station	

Interestingly in the 1897 Appendix only Wainfleet Road crossing gates are shown as worked by the signalman (West box). By 1912 Thorpe Culvert, Wainfleet, Havenhouse and Seacroft level crossings were worked by wheels in the signal boxes. The frames in all the boxes on the line were replaced in 1899-1900. Thorpe Culvert was supplied with a Saxby & Farmer frame with rocker locking in September 1899. Wainfleet (East) was equipped with a Railway Signalling Company 25-lever tappit frame in the same month. Havenhouse was given a Saxby & Farmer frame in August. Seacroft received a GNR (E1 pattern) 44-lever tappit frame in October, and in April 1900, Skegness was supplied with a Railway Signalling Company 80-lever frame with tappit locking. This replaced the Saxby & Farmer frame which had occupied the box since it opened in 1883.

Seacroft signal box and crossing. *Peter Wombwell*

Appendix Two

Operating Instructions

BRAKE POWER TO BE PROVIDED AND NUMBER OF VEHICLES TO BE ATTACHED TO PASSENGER TRAINS

SKEGNESS BRANCH (no train must exceed 18 vehicles in all.)

When without a continuous brake which is worked from the engine		*When at least one half of the vehicles of the train are fitted with a continuous brake which is worked from the engine*		*When the train is fitted throughout with a continuous brake which is worked from the engine*	
No. of carriages including brakevan	*No. of guards each with a brakevan*	*No. of carriages including brakevans*	*No. of guards each with a brake van*	*No. of carriages including brakevans*	*No. of guards each with a brakevan*
When not exceeding		*When not exceeding*		*When not exceeding*	
9	1	10	1	12	1
18	2	18	2	18	2

A pullman car or a bogie carriage to be considered equal to two ordinary vehicles.

Two horse boxes, carriage trucks, milk (trucks of 4 wheels), or fish trucks to be considered as 'one carriage'.

Three goods or cattle wagons to be considered as 'two carriages'.

Mixed trains of empty and loaded carriages must be considered as 'loaded' and goods provided accordingly.

GUARDS TO BE PROVIDED AND MAXIMUM NUMBER OF PAIRS OF WHEELS OF WHICH PASSENGER TRAINS ARE TO CONSIST (IRRESPECTIVE OF ENGINE POWER)

SKEGNESS BRANCH

PASSENGER TRAINS (Maximum pairs of wheels per train)		*EMPTY CARRIAGE AND EMPTY MILK VAN TRAINS*
Ordinary	*For one guard when the load exceeds the number of pairs of wheels shown, an additional guard to be provided*	*Except under special circumstances it is not necessary to provide more than one guard with any empty oaching stock or empty milk van train. Maximum pairs of wheels per train*
60*	45†	75

*   No express train to exceed 54 pairs of wheels
†   Maximum 45 pairs of wheels·for one guard

146

MAXIMUM SPEED AT WHICH TRAINS MAY RUN OVER CERTAIN PORTIONS
OF THE LINE

SKEGNESS BRANCH

		Maximum speed per hour
Between Firsby south and east junctions	}	Fifteen
Curve immediately ease of Wainfleet station	}	
Skegness - Down trains when passing Down home signals	}	
and over points where line diverges to	}	Ten
various platforms	}	

WHISTLING SIGNALS

Station or Junction		*No. of whistles*
Firsby station	Back of platform and Skegness branch	2 long
	Skegness branch to up main line	5
	To or from east junction	2
Firsby South Junction	To or from East Junction	2
Firsby East Junction	To or from Firsby Junction	1 long, 2 short
	To or from south junction	2
Wainfleet	Up sidings and down main line	1 long, 2 short
	Up sidings and down engine shed	1 long
	Up main line and engine shed	1 long, 2 short
	Down main line and up sidings	1 long, 1 short
Skegness	Starting from No. 1 platform line	1
	No. 1 platform line and southern group	1 long, 1 short
	No. 1 platform line and northern group	1 long, 2 short
	Starting from No. 2 platform line	2
	No. 2 platform line and southern group	2 long, 1 short
	No. 2 platform line and northern group	2 long, 2 short
	Starting from No. 3 platform line	3
	No. 3 platform line and southern group	3 long, 1 short
	No. 3 platform line and northern group	3 long, 2 short
	Starting from No. 4 platform line	4
	No. 4 platform line and southern group	4 long, 1 short
	No. 4 platform line and northern group	4 long, 2 short
	Starting from No. 5 platform line	5
	No. 5 platform line and southern group	5 long, 1 short
	No. 5 platform line and northern group	5 long, 2 short
	Starting from No. 6 platform	6
	No. 6 platform line and southern group	6 long, 1 short
	No. 6 platform line and northern group	6 long, 2 short
	Starting from No. 7 platform line	7
	No. 7 platform line and southern group	7 long, 1 short
	No. 7 platform line and northern group	7 long, 2 short

Station or Junction		*No. of whistles*
Skegness	Southern loop and No. 6 platform line	6
	Southern loop and No. 7 platform line	7
	Turntable line and southern group	1 short, 2 long
	Turntable line and northern group	2 short, 2 long
	Northern loop and No. 1 platform line	1 long, 2 short
	Northern loop and No. 2 platform line	2 long, 2 short
	Northern loop and No. 3 platform line	3 long, 2 short
	Northern loop and down sidings	1 short, 1 crow
	Northern group and northern loop	According to destination
	Southern group and northern loop	According to destination
	Down siding and southern group	1 short, 1 crow
	Down siding and up main line	1 crow
	Down siding and northern group	2 short, 1 crow
	Gasworks siding	3, pause 3
	Northern loop and turntable	2 short, 2 long
	Up main line and No. 1 platform line	1 short, 1 long
	Up main line and No. 2 platform line	2 short
	Up main line and No. 3 platform line	3 short
	Up main line and No. 4 platform line	4 short
	Up main line and turntable	2 long
	Southern group	1 long, 2 short

Unidentified classes 'J39' 0-6-0 and 'K3' 2-6-0 stand in the platforms at Skegness in the kind of weather definitely not suited to trips to the seaside, *c.* late 1940s.

P.H. Holmes Collection

Appendix Three

Skegness - Special Trains, August Bank Holiday, 1936

Train Rep No.	Train Class.	Train Type	Time	From	Route	Skegness Arr.	Skegness Return dep.	Remarks
			am			*am*	*pm*	
754	EP	ADEX	(7.48 York)	Middlesborough	Doncaster, Lincoln, Melville	10.38	10.55	7 bogies, including Buffet Car.
173	EP	HALFEX	10.00	Peterborough	Spalding	11.22	8.43	Brake Third, 6 Thirds, First, Brake Third - all 6-wheeled, non-corridor, non-lavatory. Two First class compartments to be provided and reserved for First class ticket holders. To seat 850 passengers.
Sunday, 2nd August								
756	EP	HALFEX	10.00	Grantham	Sleaford	11.28	9.24	Small, to seat 550 passengers.
218	EP	HALFEX	9.45	Nottingham Victoria	Allington Jn-Barkston East Jn	11.35	7.54	Bogie suburban set and 5 six-wheeled, non-corridor, non-lavatory Thirds.
174	EP	Additional	10.05	Gainsboro' Lea Road	Lincoln, Midville	11.43	8.06	Small, to seat 300 passengers. Two First class compartments to be provided and reserved for First class ticket holders.
219	EP	HALFEX	9.50	Nottingham Victoria	Allington Jn-Barkston East Jn	11.48	8.00	Bogie suburban set and 5 six-wheeled, non-corridor, non-lavatory Thirds.
757	EP	HALFEX		Mansfield	Pyewipe Jn, Midville	11.53	9.42	Bogie suburban set and 5 six-wheeled, non-corridor, non-lavatory Thirds.
220	EP	HALFEX	10.00	Nottingham Victoria	Allington Jn-Barkston East Jn	11.58	8.12	
						pm		
758	EP	HALFEX		Sutton-in-Ashfield C.	Pyewipe Jn, Midville	12.11	9.54	
759	EP	HALFEX		Sutton-in-Ashfield C.	Pyewipe Jn, Midville	12.22	10.06	
223	EP	HALFEX	10.05	Ilkeston	Gedling, Allington Jn-Barkston East Jn	12.28		9.12 Ordinary, to seat 850 passengers.
224	EP	HALFEX	10.00	Leicester Belgrave Rd	Allington Jn-Barkston East Jn	12.34	7.48	Bogie suburban set and 5 six-wheeled, non-corridor, non-lavatory Thirds.
205	EP	HALFEX		Hucknall Central	Pyewipe Jn, Midville	12.39	9.30	
760	EP	HALFEX		Histon (11.22 March)	Spalding	12.44	9.06	Rep. No. 755 on return.
225	EP	HALFEX	10.05	Pinxton	Gedling, Allington Jn-Barkston East Jn	12.53	7.31	
206	EP	HALFEX		Sheffield Victoria	Retford, Midville	12.58	8.18	Ordinary, to seat 800.

Train Rep No.	Train Class.	Train Type	Time	From	Route	Skegness Arr.	Return dep.	Remarks
			am			*pm*	*pm*	
207	EP	HALFEX		Deepcar	Retford, Midville	1.17		
228	EP	HALFEX	10.20	Burton-upon-Trent	Egginton Jn, Gedling, Allington Jn-Barkston East Jn		8.37	Ordinary, to seat 700.
761	EP	HALFEX	11.50	Chesterfield Mkt Pl.	Pyewipe Jn, Midville	1.22	8.31	Small, to seat 400.
762	EP	HALFEX		Newark	Barkston N. Jn, Sleaford	1.27	10.37	
88	EP	HALFEX	10.40	Kings Cross	Spalding	1.32 / 1.38	9.48 / 7.25	Vestibuled - Brake Composite non-corridor, non-lavatory, 8 Thirds non-corridor, non-lavatory and 8.45 am Buffet Car set. (Two First class compartments to be provided and reserved for First class ticket holders.) Engine will run light from Skegness to Firsby to turn and return to Skegness in time to work return Special.
229	EP	HALFEX	11.14	Derby	Gedling, Allington Jn-Barkston East Jn	1.44	9.18	Ordinary, to seat 700.
783	EP	HALFEX	10.42 / 10.48	Batley / Leeds Central}	Combined Wakefield Westgate	1.49	9.00	Each portion - Half Buffet Tourist Train E42.
763	EP	HALFEX		Clowne	Pyewipe Jn, Midville	1.59	10.49	Small, to seat 400.
764	EP	HALFEX	11.50	Branston	Sleaford West	2.09	10.00	
201	EP	HALFEX		Hull Corporation Pier	New Holland, Grimsby T., Firsby	2.21	8.23	Two First class compartments to be reserved for First class ticket holders.
766	EP	HALFEX	*pm* 12.12	Finningley	Lincoln, Midville	2.32	10.12	Small, to seat 400.
767	EP	HALFEX	12.05	Askern	Shafthome Jn, Lincoln, Midville	2.37	9.36	Brake Third corridor lavatory, 6 Saloon Thirds, Brake Composite lavatory (stock off 623 special, Yarmouth Vauxhall-Gainsborough Lea Rd, Saturday 1st August) and 6-wheeled Saloon Third (reserved for 'Rising Sun').
770	EP	HALFEX		Kettering	Bourne, Spalding	2.42	11.01	13 bogies (LMS). Booking stations - Weldon, Kettering, Desboro', Market Harborough, Kibworth, Wigston, Rearsby, Brooksby.

No.			Origin	Dep.	Route / via			Remarks
771	EP	HALFEX	Northampton		Peterboro' E. and N., Spalding	2.50	11.07	LMS stock
772	EP	HALFEX	Northampton		Peterboro' E. and N., Spalding	3.00	11.19	LMS stock.

Monday, 3rd August

No.			Origin	Dep. *am*	Route / via	*am*	*pm*	Remarks
854	EP	ADEX	Doncaster Central	5.38	Newark, Barkston North Jn, Sleaford	8.19	7.23	Buffet Tourist train E.40.
855	EP	ADEX	New Basford		Pyewipe Jn, Midville	8.24	7.11	
856	EP	ADEX	Leicester Central		Pyewipe Jn, Midville	8.38	6.55	
857	EP	ADEX	Peterboro' North	7.44	Spalding	9.09	6.26	Small, to seat 450.
858	EP	ADEX	Boston	8.40		9.15	9+27	Small, to seat 400. + Empty train to form 862 Special, 10.30 am ex-Boston.
878	EP	ADEX	Leicester Belgrave Rd	6.50	Allington Jn-Barkston east Jn	9.29	7.05 *pm*	Bogie suburban.
859	EP	ADEX	Peakirk	8.02	Spalding	9.35	6.40	Small, to seat 600.
860	EP	ADEX	Gresley		Bourne, Spalding	9.54	10.21	8 bogies (LMS). Booking stations - Melton Mowbray, Leicester, Kirby Muxloe, Bagworth, Coalville, Ashby, Moira, Gresley.
879	EP	ADEX	Derby	7.05	Gedling, Allington Jn- Barkston E. Jn }	10.02	7.36	8 vehicles
881	EP		Burton-upon-Trent	6.36	Eggington Jn }			6-wheeled non-corridor, non-lavatory Third brake, 2 six-wheeled non-corridor, non-lavatory Thirds, transferred at Derby to and from 879 Special.
861	EP	ADEX	Sheffield Victoria		Retford Straight Line, Lincoln, Midville	10.17	9.12	
862	EP	ADEX	Boston	10.30		11.05	11+30 *am*	Small, to seat 400. + Empty train.
863	EP	ADEX	Lincoln	10.23	Midville	11.39 *noon*	9.44 *pm*	Small, to seat 500.
890	EP	HALFEX	Nottingham Victoria	10.10	Allington Jn-Barkston East Jn	12.00 *noon*	7.42 *pm*	2 Bogie suburban trains, coupled.
891	EP	HALFEX	Nottingham Victoria	10.16	Allington Jn- Barkston East Jn	12.08	8.41	2 Bogie suburban trains, coupled.
892	EP	HALFEX	Nottingham Victoria	10.21	Allington Jn-Barkston East Jn	12.16	9.18	2 Bogie suburban trains, coupled.
893	EP	HALFEX	Nottingham Victoria	11.06	Allington Jn-Barkston East Jn	1.02	9.52	2 Bogie suburban trains, coupled.

Train Rep No.	Train Class.	Train Type	Time	From	Route	Skegness Arr.	Return dep.	Remarks
			am			*pm*	*pm*	
894	EP	HALFEX	11.20	Nottingham Victoria	Allington Jn - Barkston East Jn	1.16	10.04	2 Bogie suburban trains, coupled.
864	EP	HALFEX		Shirebrook North	Pyewipe Jn, Midville	1.32	9.58	
896	EP	HALFEX	11.30	Derby	Gedling, Allington Jn - Barkston East Jn	2.07	9.00	Ordinary, to sent 550.
865	EP	HALFEX		Chesterfield Mkt Pl.	Pyewipe Jn, Midville	2.23	9.38	
897	EP	HALFEX	11.40	Derby	Gedling, Allington Jn - Barkston East Jn	2.28	9.06	Ordinary, to seat 550.
867	EP	HALFEX		Conisbrough	Retford Straight Line, Lincoln Avoiding Line, Midville	2.41	9.24	Return via Lincoln station.
868	EP	HALFEX		Woodhouse	Pyewipe Jn, Midville	2.46	10.15	
870			*pm* 9†40	Boston		10†15		† Empty train after working 869 Special, 8.15 pm ex-Mablethorpe.

Explanation of abbreviations: EP - Express passenger. ADEX - Day excursion. HALFEX - Half Day Excursion.

Ex-GER class 'D15' 4-4-0 is seen at Skegness in 1936.

A.G. Ellis Collection

Skegness Departures
August Bank Holiday Sunday 1958

No.	Time	Plat.	Stations to:
574Q	5.36 pm	1	Eastville, Sibsey and Boston.
573	5.42 pm	2	Eastville, Sibsey and Boston.
572Q	6.00 pm	7	Hubberts Bridge, Swineshead, Heckington, Sleaford.
571	6.14 pm	5	All above Stations and Sleaford.
153	6.20 pm	1	Havenhouse, Wainfleet, Thorpe Culvert and Firsby.
570Q	6.30 pm	4	Lincoln Cent.
569	6.40 pm	3	Lincoln Cent.
560	6.58 pm	6	Boston, West Hallam, Derby Friargate.
564	7.10 pm	7	Basford N., Newthorpe, Eastwood & Langley Mill, Jacksdale, Pye Hill, Somercotes, Pinxton South.
155	7.22 pm	1	Eastville, Sibsey and Boston.
397	7.34 pm	5	Melton Mowbray, Thurnby, Humberstone, Leicester B. Road.
981	7.40 pm	4	Syston, Wigston Magna, Kibworth, Market Harboro', Desboro' & R., Kettering, Wellingborough (Mid Road).
562	7.46 pm	7	Boston, Daybrook, Kimberley, Awsworth, Ilkeston North.
325	7.52 pm	2	Kiveton Bridge, Killamarsh C., Renishaw C., Staveley C. & Works. Chesterfield Cent.
401	7.58 pm	6	Nottingham Victoria.
433Q	8.04 pm	3	Spalding Town and Peterborough North.
407	8.10 pm	5	Boston, Netherfield & C., Nottingham Vic., New Basford, Basford N.
623	8.16 pm	1	Lincoln C,. Gainsboro' Lea Rd., S. Elmsall, Hemsworth, Wakefield W., Ardsley and Leeds Cent.
431	8.22 pm	4	Spalding Town, Peterboro' East & North, Whittlesea.
567	8.34 pm	2	Offord, St Neots, Sandy, Biggleswade, Arlesey, Three Counties.
566	8.40 pm	6	Kirton and Spalding Town.
622	8.46 pm	7	Lincoln Cent., Gainsboro' Lea Road, Fitzwilliam, Ossett, Dewsbury, Batley, Bradford Exchange.
157	8.55 pm	1	Havenhouse, Wainfleet, Thorpe Culvert, Firsby.
565	9.07 pm	5	Leicester B. Road.
568	9.19 pm	3	Algarkirk, Surfleet, Littleworth, St James Deeping, Peakirk, Yaxley h Farcet, Holme, Huntingdon North.
321	9.31 pm	7	New Basford, Hucknall C., Sutton-in-A. Town, Skegby, Pleasley East.
320	9.43 pm	4	Boston, Bottesford, Bingham, Radcliffe-on-T, Bulwell Common, Hucknall C., Kirkby Bentinck, Tibshelf T., Pilsley, Heath.
324	9.55 pm	1	Newark (N'gate) Retford, Rossington, Stainforth, Hatfield, Thorne South.
180	10.20 pm	4	Havenhouse, Wainfleet, Thorpe Culvert, Firsby and Boston.
704	10.40 pm	6	Mickleover, Etwall, Burton-on-Trent, Gresley, Measham, Shackerstone, Market Bosworth, Stoke Golding, Nuneaton, Trent Valley.
991	11.04 pm	2	Burton-on-Trent, Swadlincote, Woodville, Moira, Ashby-de-la-Z., and Coalville Town.

Note: 'Q' Runs if required.

Appendix Five

Engine Headboards for Excursion and Additional Trains to Skegness, Mablethorpe and Cleethorpes

Locomotives working Excursion and additional trains to Cleethorpes, Mablethorpe and Skegness from Great Northern and Great Central Sections, must carry boards with numbers pasted thereon displaying the Excursion and Special Train Arrangements Circular number of the train.

In the case of trains which pass from one Section to another where more than one working number is utilised in the Excursion and Special Train Arrangements Circulars, the originating number will be displayed.

Engines working trains from the Great Eastern Section which travel via March and Spalding must, from the first-named junction, carry headboards displaying the numbers allotted in the Great Northern Section Excursion and Special Train Arrangements Circular.

With regard to trains from the LMS Company's System, when running between:

Peterboro' East or North	}	
Doncaster, Lincoln	}	
Spalding*	}	and Skegness or Mablethorpe
Nottingham Low Level	}	
Doncaster		
Lincoln	}	and Cleethorpes

the number shown in the respective Great Northern or Great Central Excursion and Special Train Arrangements Circular must be displayed.

* This instruction will also apply to trains from the M&GN Company's System to Skegness, Mablethorpe or Cleethorpes.

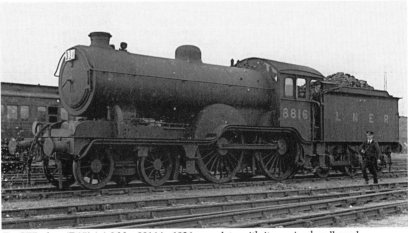

Ex-GER class 'D15' 4-4-0 No. 8816 in 1936 complete with its engine headboard.
A.G. Ellis Collection

Appendix Six

Length of Excursion and Additional Trains to Skegness, Mablethorpe and Cleethorpes

As far as practicable the length of trains, including engine, should not exceed the figures shown below :

To	Feet
Skegness	740
Mablethorpe	650
Cleethorpes	690

Immediately it becomes known that any of these lengths will be exceeded, the Superintendent, Central Timing Office, Marylebone, must be communicated with and, where necessary, a telegraphic advice despatched to District Superintendent, Lincoln and to Station Master, Skegness, Mablethorpe or Cleethorpes, as the case may be, to enable platform and stabling arrangements to be determined.

Stations attaching additional vehicles *en route* as well as depots and stations where the trains are formed must comply with these instructions.

Class 'J11' 0-6-0 No. 5223 stands in the sidings with empty excursion stock on 7th August, 1939. No. 5223 was an ex-GCR engine, built by Beyer, Peacock & Co. in 1904 and withdrawn in June 1958. *C.S. Bayes*

Appendix Seven

Butlin's Holiday Camp

Billy Butlin's first impressions of Skegness, in 1927, were not at all favourable. The whole town was so small that as he stood outside the railway station he could see cows grazing in nearby fields. However, Skegness was to become the catalyst for the biggest holiday revolution this country has ever seen.

After hearing of Skegness from two friends of his in London, Butlin determined to have a look at the place himself, (at first thinking it was in Scotland!). Catching the train at Kings Cross he headed north. The view from the train window, as it steamed north of Peterborough, was vastly different to the West Country scenery he was used to. There was more industry and more people and it gave him his first inkling of why people wanted to get away from their urban homes and factories and go to the seaside.

'We reached Lincolnshire and the character of the landscape changed, we rattled on through flat featureless fields stretching to the distance on either side. We stopped at Boston and Sleaford and tiny places with names like Hubberts Bridge and Swineshead. Was Skegness at the back of beyond? I began to have doubts about the whole idea.'

There was little to see when he arrived that eased his doubts. Skegness seemed to consist of little more than two streets and a short promenade, inappropriately called the Grand Parade. There was Lumley Road which ran from the railway station as far as the Queen Victoria Memorial Clock Tower, and High Street, which ran parallel. On one side of the clock tower there were about 20 small hotels and boarding houses, and on the other, where the road ran alongside the sand dunes, was a pier and a small wooden theatre. Butlin got to know the theatre owner, George Burrows, and together they ran several carnivals and brass band festivals. There were several stalls in this area and beyond them more sand dunes, fields, and an area known locally as 'the Jungle'.

Standing there on a wet and windy winter day Butlin tried to imagine the place in the summer. It was then that he realised that this was the place to be, Charabanc trips and the railway, also the growth of the motor car, meant that Skegness could easily become popular with day trippers and holiday makers from the teeming populations of the Midlands and North. His instincts turned out to be right, within 10 years Skegness was to be transformed into a thriving seaside resort.

In 1928 Butlin imported the first Dodgem cars from the United States and installed then at Skegness, with great success. In 1934 he began plans for a holiday camp along the lines of those he had seen in his native Canada. In 1935 he bought 40 acres of land near the seafront north of Skegness and work began on building the camp. The camp opened at Easter, 1936. The weather was unkind, it was cold and threatening to rain. Even worse the camp was still incomplete and no mains water had been laid on. Within hours it was apparent that, teething troubles apart, they were on to a winner. For just 35 shillings holiday makers had all their meals provided and were accommodated in small but comfortable chalets. There were plenty of facilities for them to enjoy, free of charge, and there was some basic entertainment for them in the evenings. Butlin's were in business .

The opening of Skegness was to be followed quickly by legislation which forced all employers to follow the lead of the enlightened and provide paid holidays for their employees. Butlin's policy was: a week's holiday for a week's pay. It was to strike the right chord with countless millions of people in Britain in the years to come.

In 1937 Butlin's became a limited company; in 1939 Skegness camp was taken over by the military becoming 'HMS Arthur' for the duration of World War II. The camp reopened in 1946, along with similar establishments at Clacton, Filey, Pwllheli and Ayr.

Billy Butlin died in Jersey in 1980, Skegness's famous 'jolly fisherman' is carved on his gravestone.

Today the camp at Skegness bears little resemblance to the cheap and cheerful place that opened its gates in 1936. It is now Butlin's Funcoast World. Many visitors come on self catering holidays, the facilities are infinitely better and the entertainment top class. The ubiquitous Redcoats are still there and above all the atmosphere generated in those early years is still much in evidence.

The interesting monorail system installed at a cost of £120,000 in the early 1960s was the first of its kind in the country. The one mile long circuit is 16 feet above ground level with two stations, one in the north and the other the south. One is next to, and level with, the upper floor of Huckleberry's Showbar. The second station serves the Amusement Park and other amenities in the north of the camp. The platforms, on the outside of the circuit, are reached by stairs. The location of the stations has been altered over the years, for example the original north station was a few yards away from the present structure, having a platform on the inside of the circuit, it now serves as a maintenance point.

Two trains are operated with a third on standby if required. These run in an anti-clockwise direction, according to demand, between March and the end of October. Each train consists of a driving carriage at each end which seat nine passengers, and two middle carriages, each seating 10 passengers, a total of 38 passengers per train, with no standing. The monorail is one of the free amenities on the camp. The loading and unloading of passengers and train movements are supervised by members of staff at each station. At present the sliding doors on the right hand side of the trains are manually operated, being locked and opened from the outside; at some future date it is hoped to have air-operated doors controlled by the driver.

Each train body rests upon six bogies which have four solid rubber tyres each. The original trains were powered by three five horsepower motors but, due to problems with synchronising these, by 1966, a single vertical drive 15 horsepower motor had been developed. As technology improved over the subsequent years, this was gradually developed and modified on site. The current for the electrical motor is collected from copper wires running alongside the rail by using a British Rail type collector and brush system. The brakes were hydraulic but are now of the air-assisted disc type.

The bodywork of the trains was originally constructed of glass fibre over a wooden frame, but due to the gradual rotting of the wood and the expensive nature of glass fibre replacement, the present trains, built by Rundle of New Bolingbroke, are constructed of steel panels around a steel frame, thus enabling parts to be replaced quickly and economically. The new trains are higher than the old ones, 5 ft 11 in. inside.

The driver operates 'tram like' controls including a 'dead man's handle'. Trains can reach a maximum speed of around 12 mph but, due to the short distance between the stations, the average speed is considerably less. Trains can be operated in multiple should a breakdown occur, the multiple operating equipment being carried on board. This type of manoeuvre is effected only in the case of breakdowns. Signalling is operated automatically by a trip system being activated by the trains themselves. When a signal is passed the switch is tripped, setting it to red. It is then set to green when the next signal is passed, allowing the other train to proceed.

At the end of the season the carriages and bogies are individually hoisted from the rail by crane. All wheel bearings are changed and the bodywork thoroughly checked for faults and wear. Following an extensive check of the rail itself and after a further examination of the trains they are lifted back in place.

The following is a LNER memorandum from 1947 concerning proposals for the bus station which was eventually built next to the railway station at Skegness.

LONDON & NORTH EASTERN RAILWAY

Memorandum to the   20th February, 1947
Traffic, Works and Locomotive Committee

Skegness Bus Station for Messrs Butlin's Holiday Camp Traffic

Messrs Butlin's Holiday Camp at Skegness was first opened in 1936 with accommodation for 2,000 persons. Extensions were made in 1937, 1938 and 1939, bringing the total capacity to 5,500. The proprietors are now engaged upon further extensions which will enable 8,000 people to be accommodated for holidays alone and in addition, amusement facilities on a large scale are being provided which should enable us to secure considerable excursion traffic from the West Riding, South Yorkshire, the Midlands, Humberside, etc.

Messrs Butlin's have always encouraged their holiday visitors to travel by rail and have planned their patrons' journeys with us. Prior to the war 85 per cent of the visitors arrived at Skegness by rail.

The anticipated growth of passenger traffic at Skegness during the holiday season, will require a number of major improvements to the layout and signalling as well as modernisation of the station buildings.

The Camp site is approximately three miles from the railway station and all traffic between the two points is conveyed by road services. At the present time facilities for effecting the satisfactory transfer of traffic from one service to another do not exist. It is, therefore, proposed as the first step in the modernisation scheme to erect an Omnibus Station on land owned by the Company and adjoining the Passenger station where the transfer of passengers can proceed expeditiously and under cover.

The work, which it is hoped to have completed by the 1947 Holiday Season, includes the following main features:

1. Two covered platforms - one 150 ft long, to accommodate up to five double-decker 'buses at one time, and intended to deal with traffic ARRIVING FROM Messrs Butlin's Camp, and another 200 ft long, to accommodate up to 6 double-decker 'buses at a time and intended to be used by 'buses taking passengers TO the Camp.
2. A luggage depot, sited between the platforms, provided with the necessary racks and counters, and with access for lorries. (Messrs Butlin's will provide staff to man the luggage counters.)
3. Separate lavatory accommodation for incoming and outgoing passengers to ensure complete segregation of the two streams of traffic.
4. Covered approach from railway station to the 'bus station.
5. Suitable gates between the railway station and the 'bus station, also at the entrance to and exit from the 'bus station; traffic direction signs, movable barriers and adequate lighting.
6. Consequential alterations to the Coal Yard accommodation, including a new entrance from Richmond Drive, south of the abattoir.

The estimated cost of the scheme is £12,503 gross, £12,453 net, made up as follows:

CHIEF ENGINEER

	£	£
Structural work, etc.	11,541	
LESS value of materials recoverable	50	11,491

CHIEF ELECTRICAL ENGINEER
Lighting   962
                                                       12,453

The estimated original capital cost of works displaced is £837 and there would be additional charges for maintenance and renewals amounting to £270 pa.
It is RECOMMENDED that authority be given for an expenditure of £12,503.

(signed) C.H. NEWTON

(Initialed) V.M. B.-W.

Tenders were invited. The one from Tersons Ltd, Builders & Contractors, 1, Seward Street, Goswell Road, London EC1, for £11,470. 3s. 9d. was accepted on 8th April, 1949 and they were awarded the contract.

The head of the memorandum also carries a handwritten entry: 'What is traffic worth? - £123,000'.

PRO reference: RAIL/390/1292

Immaculate class 'B1' 4-6-0 No. 61179 of Top Shed waits to take the 8.06 am train to Skegness (arrival time 11.09 am), on 9th June, 1962.   *R.F. Orpwood*

Acknowledgements

History of the Great Northern Railway, C.H. Grinling (Methuen, 1898)
The Great Northern Railway, (3 Volumes) John Wrottesley (Batsford, 1979)
Great Northern Steam, W.A. Tuplin (Ian Allan, 1971)
Great Northern Locomotive History, (3 Volumes) N. Groves (RCTS 1986-92)
Locomotives of the LNER, (Parts 3A, 3B, 5, 6A, 7) (RCTS)
The Engineer, GNR Supplement, 1913
A History of the Fens of South Lincolnshire, W.H. Wheeler (Watkins 1900)
London & North Eastern Railway Magazine, September 1935
Eastern Region Magazine, November 1961
Lincs, Notts and Derbyshire by Rail (Jarrold 1989)
South East Lincolnshire Travellers Association (SELTA) newsletters
Lincolnshire and East Yorkshire Transport Review
The Gresley Observer (Gresley Society)
Great Northern Railway Society
The Lincoln, Rutland & Stamford Mercury
The Lincolnshire Chronicle
The East Lincolnshire Railway, A.J. Ludlam (The Oakwood Press, 1991)
The Lincolnshire Loop, GNR, and the River Witham, A.J. Ludlam (The Oakwood Press, 1995)
The Spilsby to Firsby Railway, A.J. Ludlam (The Oakwood Press, 1985)
The New Line, Stephen Walker (KMS 1985)
Firsby to Wainfleet & Skegness Stephen Walker (KMS 1987)
Steam Days, January 1996 and March 1996 issues
Back Track, Volume 8, No. 3
Hello Campers, Sue Read and Brian Haynes (Bantam, 1986)
The Lincolnshire Archives
Public Record Office, Kew
Wainfleet Museum

H.A. Bloy
Alan Burkitt
Charles Burkitt
Cyril Clark
Norman Clark
Godfrey Croughton
Algy Epton
Frank Gelder
Geoff Goslin

Peter Grey
Peter Holmes
R. Hudson
Winston Kime
Don Leary
Lawson Little
Steve Priestley
Alan Rundle

David Robinson
Richard Scupholm
Stewart Squires
Doreen Teesdale
John Thornley
Jim Walker
Barrie Wilkinson
Peter Wombwell

and many others who took the trouble to help.